Rawls
A Beginner's Guide

ONEWORLD BEGINNER'S GUIDES combine an original, inventive, and engaging approach with expert analysis on subjects ranging from art and history to religion and politics, and everything in-between. Innovative and affordable, books in the series are perfect for anyone curious about the way the world works and the big ideas of our time.

Rawls
A Beginner's Guide

Paul Graham

ONEWORLD

A Oneworld Book

First published as *Rawls: Oneworld Thinkers* by Oneworld Publications, 2007
This edition published by Oneworld Publications, 2016

ISBN 978-1-78074-811-5
eISBN 978-1-78074-812-2

Typeset by Jayvee, Trivandrum, India
Printed and bound in Great Britain by Clays Ltd, St Ives plc

Oneworld Publications
10 Bloomsbury Street
London WC1B 3SR
England

Contents

Preface

John Rawls's *A Theory of Justice* (1971) is one of the most influential books in moral and political philosophy published within the last one hundred years. It is read not just by philosophers, but also by those working in the fields of political science, law and social policy. His later works – *Political Liberalism* (1993) and *The Law of Peoples* (1999) – further expand his audience, as they raise issues of importance to theologians, particularly those working in the field of comparative religion, and to theorists of international relations. The aim of this book is to provide a comprehensive commentary on Rawls, extending from his earliest articles from the 1950s, to work published just before his death in 2002 and to writings that have appeared posthumously. Although his books and articles cross disciplinary boundaries in terms of their relevance, there is a focus to Rawls's work that distinguishes him from many other philosophers: he was concerned above all with the fair distribution of goods in society. Those goods are not simply material resources, such as income, but also freedom and political power. This concern with distributive justice, while seemingly narrow, opens up many important debates. These include: debates about the nature of the goods to be distributed; the relationship between freedom, equality and efficiency; gender relations; the moral justification of political principles and the problems of justifying such principles in a culturally and religiously diverse society; the conflict between moral autonomy and state coercion; and issues of global justice and human rights.

While Rawls's work is of great relevance to politics and society, it is expressed in language that may appear excessively abstract and at times daunting. There is a danger that a reader interested in questions of distributive justice will become disillusioned. I have tried to strike a balance between on the one hand clarifying and in places simplifying Rawls's arguments, and on the other engaging with the complexities of his thought. I have also balanced exegesis and criticism: readers want to know what *Rawls* argued, not what a commentator thinks Rawls *should* have said. However, a good part of Rawls's importance lies in the debates which he sparked, and much can be gained by exploring critical perspectives on Rawls. Through these critical perspectives I have attempted to convey my view of his arguments and of his ultimate significance as a political philosopher.

In writing this book I have benefited from the support and intellectual stimulation given by my former students and colleagues at Glasgow University, most especially Michael Lessnoff. Since the publication of the first edition in 2007 I have moved to Buckingham University. Given that Buckingham was founded on free market, libertarian ideas this has provided an interesting environment in which to discuss Rawls's 'left liberal' – egalitarian – ideas. I would like to acknowledge in particular the support given to me by Martin Ricketts. In addition, my teachers at the London School of Economics, where I was a graduate student, have shaped my ideas. The guidance provided by Oneworld has been invaluable. Victoria Roddam, Mark Hopwood and Martha Jay assisted me with the first edition, and Mike Harpley has helped me with the second edition. Finally, the encouragement of my parents, Douglas and Heather Graham, has been essential to the pursuit of my studies in political philosophy, and for that I am grateful.

A comment on the texts: all references are to the first edition of *A Theory of Justice*, which was published in the United States in 1971 and in the United Kingdom in 1972. As I shall argue, Rawls revised his ideas over subsequent decades and these changes were incorporated in a second edition of the book, published in 1999. Because I want to explain how his ideas changed I have decided to continue to reference the first edition. (It should be noted that the first edition was reissued in 2005.)

1
Life and work

When John Rawls died aged 81 in November 2002, the obituaries in the major newspapers were surprisingly extensive. Surprising because Rawls was not a public intellectual. All who knew him stressed his shyness, modesty and determined avoidance of publicity. Rare were his interventions in current events. He gave only one personal interview in the course of his career, and that was to a small student magazine. He was reluctant to accept awards. But although the audience for his work has largely been confined to the academic world, the impact therein was of such a scale that by the time of his death glimmers of awareness of his significance had broken through to the wider world. His most important work – *A Theory of Justice* (1971) – has sold over 250,000 copies, and been translated into twenty languages. This book on Rawls is one more addition to a huge secondary literature, amounting to an estimated 5,000 works. Who then was John Rawls?

Rawls wrote *A Theory of Justice* during an unusually unstable period in American history – at the height of the Vietnam War, and towards the end of the struggle for civil rights in the Deep South. Yet there is no direct reflection on these events in the book, and except for a brief footnote reference to Martin Luther King this holds even for his discussion of civil disobedience (Rawls 1972: 364*n*). It is true that as a professor at Harvard

University he identified himself with the anti-war movement, but this activity, while not inconsistent with his writings, appears quite separate from them. Only towards the end of his life did he comment on a concrete political event, condemning, on the fiftieth anniversary, the atomic bombing of Nagasaki and Hiroshima (Rawls 1999b: 565–72). The point is that biography is not essential to understanding Rawls's work. This contrasts with the cases where biography is helpful and illuminating (Wittgenstein), or essential (Nietzsche). However, readers coming to Rawls for the first time may find a personal sketch of the man useful in humanizing what could appear a dry argument, although the word 'dry' is a mischaracterization of work that addresses fundamentally important political questions in an intellectually imaginative way, and that has generated a series of major philosophical debates. In writing this sketch I have relied upon accounts of those who knew and were influenced by him, such as Thomas Nagel and Martha Nussbaum, as well as an obituary by Ben Rogers, who in 1999 had interviewed Rawls's friends and colleagues. In addition, since the publication of the first edition of this book there has appeared in print Rawls's 1942 undergraduate senior thesis – 'A Brief Inquiry into the Meaning of Sin and Faith' – together with a brief piece, entitled 'On my Religion', which was written in 1997 and intended largely for family and friends rather than wider circulation. I will say a few things about the former in Chapter 8, but the latter essay is of direct biographical interest.

Rawls was born the second of five brothers in Baltimore (Maryland). His father had established himself as a highly successful tax lawyer and constitutional expert, while his mother was active in Democratic Party politics and campaigned for voting rights for women. While not part of the Deep South, Maryland was a part of the former Confederacy, and according to at least one obituary Rawls's father, William Lee Rawls, shared the racial bigotry of his time and place. For John Rawls, the slavery of the South and the failure after the Civil War to grant effective rights to black Americans became the paradigm of injustice. Thomas Nagel describes Rawls's background as that of an upper-class Southerner, and other commentators have suggested that as well as discomfort at the slavery heritage of his home state, he had a powerful sense of the contingency of life – the sense that 'there but for the grace of God go I'. Natural assets, such as good heath and intelligence, and socially acquired assets, such as a privileged upbringing, combine to give some people very significant advantages in life. Rawls felt that how we organize society should ameliorate rather than exacerbate natural disadvantage. Although in later revisions of his work he pulled away from this claim, in the first edition of *A Theory of Justice* he describes natural assets as a social resource to be used for the advantage of the least well-off, and any differences in income and other resources enjoyed by the wealthy are not *deserved*, for nobody creates his or her natural assets – not even the propensity to work hard (Rawls 1972: 311–12).

After Kent School, a private establishment in Connecticut, Rawls entered Princeton University. While he had only a conventional religious upbringing, during his last two years at Princeton (1941–42) he became deeply religious and considered entering a seminary to train as a minister of religion, but decided to wait: 'I could not convince myself that my motives were sincere, and anyway I felt I should serve in the armed services as so many of my friends and classmates were doing' (Rawls 2009: 261). After completing his degree one semester early he joined the US Army as an infantryman, and was posted to New Guinea and the Philippines. He was later to say that the Second World War overshadowed everything he had done as a student, and stimulated his interest in politics (Rogers 2002). His religious convictions changed in the last year of the war and he ceased to be orthodox (to use his own expression).

Although he suggests it is difficult to explain why this change took place he does mention three incidents. In December 1944, after his Company had secured the ridge overlooking the town of Limon on the island of Leyte, the Lutheran Pastor gave a sermon in which he said that 'God aimed our bullets at the Japanese while [He] protected us from theirs' (Rawls 2009: 262). The statement angered Rawls, who challenged the chaplain for propagating a clear falsehood about divine providence. A second incident was the death of a comrade who was killed on lookout. The First Sergeant had sought a volunteer to give blood for a wounded soldier and another to go on reconnaissance. Rawls had the right blood type. As he says: 'I was quite disconsolate and couldn't get the incident out of my mind … I don't know why this incident so affected me, other than my fondness for Deacon, as death was a common occurrence' (Rawls, 2009: 262). The third incident was seeing the films of Allied forces liberating the concentration camps in Germany. These incidents – and especially the third – made him question the existence of God: 'to interpret history as expressing God's will, God's will must accord with the most basic ideas of justice as we know them. For what else can the most basic justice be?' (Rawls 2009: 263).

While he abandoned orthodox Christianity, unlike many political philosophers, who, to use Max Weber's phrase are 'religiously unmusical', Rawls nonetheless retained a feel for religious belief and experience. One of the motivations for a shift in his work between the 1970s and the 1990s was the attempt to correct what he regarded as a defect in *A Theory of Justice*, namely that it relied on a conception of human agency and rationality which a reasonable Christian or Muslim might reject. The way we defend principles of justice must not rely on 'sectarian' humanist premises – it should be possible for reasonable Jews, Christians, Muslims, atheists and those of many other beliefs to embrace the just society. His discussion of, for example,

abortion, while concluding there should be a right to it, is
sensitive both to religious and secular arguments for its prohibi-
tion, recognizing that the dispute over the status of the unborn
child may never be resolved (Rawls 1999a: 169–71). And he
concludes his reflections in 'On my Religion' with a defence
of human reason that both theists and non-theists can embrace:
'God's being, however great the divine powers, does not determine the essential canons of reason … (and) the content of the
judgments of practical reason depends on social facts about how
humans are related in society and to one another … and this is so
even if these facts are themselves the outcome of God's creation'
(Rawls, 2009: 268).

After the war Rawls undertook a doctorate in philosophy,
with a thesis on ethical decision-making. Some philosophers
switch from one paradigm to another, and sometimes from one
set of philosophical interests to another. Rawls is remarkably
consistent in his interests, and changes in his arguments were
gradual, rather than being seismic shifts. Rawls's preferred outlet
for the initial publication of his ideas was the journal article, and
in 1999 all his articles were brought together in a single volume,
Collected Papers. There are twenty-six articles and an interview.
This is not a *huge* output for a career that spanned fifty years,
but the articles he did publish appeared in the most prestigious
journals and often provoked an immediate debate, even before
they reappeared in revised form in his books. In the twenty-
year period before the publication of *A Theory of Justice*, particularly notable articles include his second one, 'Two Concepts of
Rules' (1955), which has been very influential in debates about
punishment, 'Legal Obligation and the Duty of Fair Play' (1964)
and 'The Justification of Civil Disobedience' (1969), which, as
the titles suggest, are concerned with the closely related issues
of political obligation and civil disobedience. During this time
Rawls studied or worked at Oxford (1952–3), Cornell, Harvard
and the Massachusetts Institute of Technology, before finally

settling at Harvard again. He spent the rest of his career in the Philosophy Department there.

The 1950s and 1960s are often portrayed as the dog days of moral and political philosophy. Under the influence of the late work of Ludwig Wittgenstein it was thought that moral concepts and arguments derived their validity from the contexts in which they are used: there were language games in which people moved words around as if they were pieces on a board, and the words only had meaning by reference to the game. Furthermore, the same words could be used in different ways, such that the meaning of a word depended on context and not upon any essence. For example, the word 'game' itself might carry connotations of winning or losing, of rules, of competition, but none of these need be present every time the word is used. There are, at best, 'family resemblances' or overlap between different employments of the word. Applying this to moral language, terms such as good and bad, right and wrong, justice and fairness have meaning only in particular contexts, with the consequence that 'theories' are simply moves in a game. A theory only has influence on people if it causes them to act in some way. It is emotive rather than cognitive. A consequence was that the dominant meta-ethical theories of this period – a meta-ethical theory being one that attempts to explain the meaning of moral language – were ordinary language philosophy and emotivism. It would not be crude to say that ordinary language philosophy amounted to a cataloguing exercise: everyday usage of words like good and bad were listed and compared. Emotivists claimed moral communication was the expression of emotional states. The dominant *ethical* theories – that is, theories about what we should actually do – were utilitarianism in its various forms and intuitionism which, unlike eighteenth century versions, did not depend on metaphysical claims about a moral sense, but proposed the idea that we judge right and wrong by making intuitive judgements (eighteenth-century intuitionism was a meta-ethical rather than an ethical theory). Given the scepticism about moral objectivity engendered by the meta-ethical theories of ordinary language philosophy and emotivism, it is not surprising that utilitarianism and intuitionism were the dominant ethical theories. Utilitarianism requires minimal reliance on metaphysical claims about the nature of the human agent and the structure of reason, and intuitionism is a complete abandonment of metaphysical claims.

The development of Rawls's work up to 1971 has to be seen in the context of these philosophical trends. Only gradually, and tentatively, does he break with them. The idea of reflective equilibrium relies strongly on an appeal to intuition and there is a strong, and explicit, utilitarian basis to Rawls's 1955 article 'Two Concepts of Rules' (see Rawls 1999b: 33–46). Whereas in 1955 Rawls sets out to defend utilitarianism, in *A Theory of Justice* he condemns it for failing to take seriously the separateness of persons, and regards both it and intuitionism as prime targets. Inspired in large part by Rawls's theory of justice, Kantianism, which relies on a complex conception of human agency and practical reason, once again became fashionable, as did the idea of building theories, which while respectful of the capacity of ordinary people to make moral judgements entailed a challenge to everyday moral beliefs. Using his own phrase, Rawls's work can be characterized as an exercise in 'realistic utopianism': he aims to uncover possibilities for social and political change latent in everyday experience. This is not a pure utopianism, disconnected from historical experience, but it is reformative.

Thomas Nagel, whose work bears important affinities to Rawls's, dedicated his main work on political theory, *Equality and Partiality* (Nagel 1991), to 'John Rawls, who changed the subject'. To knowing readers, that dedication carries a double meaning: Rawls changed the discipline of political philosophy, and he did so by changing its topic from a parochial concern with the meaning of moral terms to the framing of a big question: what constitutes a fair distribution of the benefits and burdens of social co-operation? The answers he provides in *A Theory of Justice* generated a variety of debates among political philosophers, and while the claim that he brought political philosophy back from the dead may be an exaggeration, he did fundamentally change its central preoccupation. It may be too early to assess the historical significance of the book, but it does have the makings of a great work in moral and political theory, comparable to Thomas Hobbes's *Leviathan* or John Stuart Mill's *On Liberty*. Stylistically, it has come in for a great deal of criticism, with commentators arguing that Rawls simply stitched together earlier journal articles. However, while it is fair to say that *A Theory of Justice* is not an easy read, it does have a relatively clear structure: three parts, nine chapters and 87 sections. The first part outlines the theory, the second part develops the derivation of the principles of justice and the third part focuses on questions of rationality and motivation. And, as Rogers suggests, Rawls was 'a phrasemaker – as well as an idea-forger – of brilliance' (Rogers 2002). The glossary of this book is full of phrases that Rawls invented: 'original position', 'veil of ignorance', 'difference principle' and so on. Furthermore, as many commentators have observed, all Rawls's book have excellent indexes – his skill at constructing indexes may have its origins in work carried out as a research student on the indexes to Walter Kaufmann's English translations of Nietzsche's writings (incidentally, Kaufmann also influenced Rawls's understanding of Nietzsche and 'perfectionism').

Rawls had modest expectations for *A Theory of Justice* and was amazed by the impact it made. Certainly, the work did not emerge from nowhere, for its main arguments had been trailed in journal articles, and mimeographed drafts of the book had been circulating among graduate students, many of whom were holding academic posts in other universities by the early 1970s. Nonetheless, the work was unexpectedly successful. It is interesting to speculate what Rawls might have gone on to write had the book been merely a modest success. He had planned to write a book on moral psychology, but instead was forced to defend his theory of justice. Since, in my view, the most important and enduring questions raised by Rawls's work concern his conception of human motivation, a book on moral psychology might have been the natural next step in the development of his work. As it was, his energies were somewhat dissipated by having to defend the many claims he makes in his book, and eventually he shifted the basis of his argument away from an (underdeveloped) Kantianism to a form of relativism, which dispensed with the Kantian conception of the human agent.

Rawls's significance must be understood, at least in part, as a consequence of the reaction to his theory of justice. And to an extent, the development of his work after *A Theory of Justice* was dictated by critiques of it. In later chapters of this book – especially Chapters 5 and 6 – I try to capture something of the debates generated by Rawls's theory. The reactions to the theory came in waves, with the first ones being a sympathetic response from the social democratic left, and hostility from the Marxist left and libertarian right. In his book Rawls sets out two principles of justice, the first of which is intended to guarantee each individual a basic set of equal liberties, and the second ensuring that in terms of material resources the worst-off are as well-off as possible. Given the need for incentives to produce, the second principle will almost certainly result in an unequal distribution of income. The second principle caught the attention of social democrats, because it provided a response to the trickle-down argument of the New Right. Appealing to empirical economic evidence, such as the Laffer Curve, New Right thinkers argued that high taxes harmed the poor, for the wealthy stopped working, emigrated or at the very least engaged in tax avoidance measures such as putting capital into off-shore funds. By cutting the top rate of income tax economic activity was stimulated, thus creating more jobs at all levels of pay and increasing the tax yield. This benefited the poor. Social democrats could concede that income differentials might be productive, but they used Rawls's argument to demonstrate that such differentials were morally justified if and only if they did indeed make the worst-off as well-off as possible.

While social democrats found intellectual support in *A Theory of Justice*, Marxists saw Rawls as a defender of capitalist inequality. Although he argued his theory was neutral between capitalist and socialist forms of economic organization, maintaining the two principles could be realized under either system, two aspects of his theory point to a tacit endorsement of capitalism. First, his efficiency argument assumes that people are strongly motivated by self-interest. Second, the fact that the first principle (equal liberty) takes priority over the second (difference principle) limits the extent to which wealth can be redistributed. Although the Marxist critique became more muted after the 1980s, in part because Rawlsian liberalism looked highly egalitarian set against the theories of the now dominant New Right (or 'neoliberals'), there continues to be Marxian (if not Marxist) criticism of his work, and in one of his last works Rawls himself doubted the principles of justice could be realized in a welfare state capitalist society. What is required is a redistribution of productive assets (Rawls 2001: 135–8).

Rawls was also attacked from the right, by libertarians such as his fellow Harvard philosopher Robert Nozick. In his book *Anarchy, State, and Utopia* (1974) Nozick defends a minimal state – that is, a state whose functions are restricted to policing – against the extensive state, which he believes would be required by Rawls's theory of justice. Nozick argues that Rawls's principles of justice entail continual interference in individuals' free choice. The appearance of *Anarchy, State, and Utopia* gave rise to a rather neat left-right debate, and seemed to reflect in philosophical debate what was going on in the real world of politics.

In the United States the consensus around the state intervention-ist policies of the 1930s New Deal and the 1960s Great Society was breaking down, with Ronald Reagan providing the politi-cal leadership for a movement that advocated a much smaller state and greater personal responsibility. In Britain the post-war welfare state settlement was challenged by Margaret Thatcher. However, despite the apparent affinity between philosophical debate and political events, Rawls's and Nozick's books were different not simply in their substantive proposals, but also in their aims. While Nozick's was superficially more readable, and indeed quite entertaining, it was less philosophically sophisti-cated than Rawls's. The justification for the minimal state was thin, resting as it did on the assertion that we have natural rights to private property, and these rights create severe restraints on what the state can require of us.

Rawls's theory of justice has two aspects: a method for deriv-ing principles, and an account of what would be derived were we to follow that method. During the 1980s Rawls made rela-tively modest changes to the principles themselves, but he made significant revisions to the method. Rawls describes his method for deriving principles as contractarian: rational agents choose principles in a hypothetical situation in which they are free and equal. Some commentators argued that this method relied on an implausible or even incoherent conception of human agency, and this criticism was at the centre of what became termed the 'communitarian-individualist' debate of the 1980s (it was some-times dubbed the 'communitarian-liberal' debate, but many communitarians resisted this, claiming they were offering an alternative liberal theory). Michael Sandel's book *Liberalism and the Limits of Justice* (1982) was the most influential communitar-ian critique, although in a later reissue (1998) he disowns that label. Sandel argues that Rawls projects a thin, individualistic and asocial model of human agency and human relationships.

Sandel's critique is ambiguous, for on the one hand he maintains that Rawls's theory is incoherent, but on the other he claims that we – meaning, Americans – 'live Rawls'. The pathologies of contemporary America, including the atomism and decline of social capital summed up in the title of Robert Putnam's book *Bowling Alone*, are theorized by Rawls. Although there was a strong whiff of conservatism about the communitarian critique, interestingly enough, a similar type of critique was advanced by feminists, who objected not only to some of the implications of the two principles, especially the apparent exclusion of the family from the scope of justice, but also to the ethic of impartiality which underlay Rawls's contractarianism. Such an ethic was masculinist and marginalized female moral experience, which manifested itself in 'caring'.

Rawls was always generous in citing those who had criticized his work, or made contributions to the development of his argument. But he also had a tendency to relegate responses to footnotes, and his reaction to communitarian and feminist criticisms of his method exemplifies this. I would argue that, although not adequately acknowledged by Rawls, the most significant developments in his work were a reaction to the criticisms of his model of the human moral agent. Through the 1980s Rawls developed a new way of understanding the derivation of the principles of justice. He did not jettison any of the concepts set out in *A Theory of Justice*, but rather introduced new concepts which force us to reinterpret the old ones. The new position is summed up, slogan-like, in the title of an influential article from 1985: 'Justice as Fairness: Political not Metaphysical'. His revisions came together in book form with the publication of *Political Liberalism* (Rawls 1996; first published 1993). Rawls's final position was much less Kantian and drew more on the tradition of religious toleration that had developed in Europe after the Wars of Religion – that is, after 1648 – and was instrumental in the formation of the United States. In some ways, the late Rawls is much more *American*. These motifs may have been present in the earlier work, but Rawls's later argument is couched more explicitly in terms of constitutional reasoning and the need to find common ground among diverse religious and cultural groups. It is not so much the object of Rawls's concern – the fact of pluralism – which gives his argument a peculiarly American tone, for European societies must address religious and cultural pluralism, but the style of argumentation. Rawls's two great heroes were Immanuel Kant and Abraham Lincoln, but it is the life and policies of the latter that predominate in *Political Liberalism*.

In 1995 Rawls suffered the first of a series of strokes, making work difficult. However, with determined effort he completed *The Law of Peoples*, which was an expansion of an earlier article. Rawls was mainly concerned with domestic justice – the relationship between the individual and the state, and relations between citizens under a state – rather than international justice, which is concerned with interstate relations. However, international politics raises moral challenges for domestic politics: citizens must assess when it is appropriate for their state to intervene in the affairs of another, and whether there are obligations on them to transfer wealth to other societies. What surprised some commentators, aware of Rawls's theory of domestic justice, was the conservatism and inegalitarianism of the law of peoples: non-liberal societies – what Rawls calls decent (hierarchical) peoples – could be part of a society of peoples, and the obligation to transfer wealth to other peoples is limited to that which is necessary to ensure the basic conditions for entry to a society of peoples. Beyond that minimum, societies must be responsible for their own wealth generation and distribution.

For many years *A Theory of Justice* was Rawls's only published book. This was followed by *Political Liberalism* in 1993. Since then there has been a flood of books under his name. These have included a new version of *A Theory of Justice* (Rawls 1999c); a shorter restatement of the theory (Rawls 2001); as mentioned above, an exploration of international justice (Rawls 1999a); a collection of all his journal articles (Rawls 1999b); and his lectures on moral philosophy (Rawls 2000). And as mentioned earlier his undergraduate thesis – which obviously was never intended for publication – has posthumously appeared in print (Rawls 2009). The lectures on moral philosophy are particularly important, for they cast light on the central problem of moral and political philosophy: the motivation for acting morally. The book is based on the final version of what Rawls regarded as his introductory course on ethics for undergraduates at Harvard, the character of which changed over the period 1977–91, as Kant's ethics became its focus. Although Rawls is remembered as a contemporary political philosopher, developing his own ideas, these lectures reveal an appreciation of the history of moral philosophy. He claimed to pose the problems of the philosophers he discussed 'as they themselves saw them, given what their understanding of these problems was in their own time' and argued that they were 'smarter than [he] was' (Rawls 2000: xvi): if there was a mistake in their arguments he supposed that they must have seen it too and have dealt with it. Their solution might be historical – their problems are not our problems – or perhaps there was part of the text (or other texts) which he – Rawls – had not read. Despite this typically modest reluctance to impose his concepts onto the thought of past philosophers, the lectures, both in the problems they pose and the interpretation of the material, do bear the influence of Rawls, and are very useful in getting a sense of the intellectual influences on his 'own' work.

As I said at the beginning of this chapter Rawls avoided reflecting on political events and, as Nagel argues, 'there is never a breath of personal information' in the work published in his lifetime (Nagel 1999: 36). However, Rawls did occasionally intervene in issues of public policy and while he declined most honours, he accepted one from President Bill Clinton: the National Humanities Medal (1999). The citation, as well as recognizing the importance of his published work, noted that 'he trained many of the generation who are now the most distinguished practitioners of moral and political philosophy, and through his mentorship he has helped many women into the ranks of a male-dominated field'. He also contributed to the so-called Philosophers' Brief, which was filed as an *amicus curiae* with the American Supreme Court in support of physician-assisted suicide (or, more accurately, in support of a lower court's ruling that statutes passed by the states of Washington and New York outlawing physician-assisted suicide were unconstitutional). Dubbed by critics a 'liberal dream team', the six philosophers who wrote the brief were, in addition to Rawls, Ronald Dworkin, Thomas Nagel, Robert Nozick, Thomas Scanlon and Judith Jarvis Thomson. Dworkin, the lead member of the team, commented that he knew of 'no other occasion on which a group has intervened in Supreme Court litigation solely as general philosophers' (Dworkin 1997: 41).

Despite this interesting intervention in American legal discourse, it is important not to see Rawls as a party thinker, that is, as someone championing a particular position on the political spectrum. As a philosopher, Rawls's objectives were different to those of a politician. A politician is concerned to construct a coalition of support around a particular set of policies. He can have an influence independently of whether his arguments are valid: to win an election you do not have to win arguments, but votes. Of course, you can go to a higher level, and distinguish politicians from statesmen. The latter are concerned with more than winning an election; they seek to establish durable political institutions, and inculcate long-term values (Rawls 1999a: 97). In American history, Rawls's hero Abraham Lincoln was, by this definition, a statesman. In Lincoln's case, it took a civil war to end slavery, and only gradually were the wounds of that war on the body politic healed. Political philosophers are neither politicians nor statesmen: it is not the fact of agreement around a set of principles that is of prime importance, but the nature of reasons for endorsing those principles. Although Rawls, Dworkin, Nagel, Nozick, Scanlon and Thomson came together in defence of a particular legal position and in broad terms set out shared reasons in support of that position, when we dig deeper we find significant moral–philosophical differences between them. It is these differences that are at the heart of philosophical discourse, and that I explore in this book.

Further reading

In addition to Nagel (1999) and Rogers (2002), see also Nussbaum (2001).

2

Justice

The title of Rawls's book, *A Theory of Justice*, may seem anodyne but in fact reveals considerable ambition. The focus, as suggested by the title, is justice, or more precisely distributive justice. Is it possible to criticize the existing distribution of resources in society? If so, how do we go about deciding what is a fairer distribution? What, in fact, *is* fair? Up for distribution are not only tangible things such as income, but also less tangible goods, like freedom and political power. Because Rawls's theory is complex we need a way of making its presentation manageable, and Rawls suggests we distinguish the *method* for deriving principles of distributive justice from the *content* of those principles (Rawls 1972: 15). While the distinction should not be drawn too sharply, it is a useful one and it largely influences the organization of this book. The aim of this chapter is to provide a wide-angle view of Rawls's theory of justice, and to locate Rawls within the history of political thought.

Rawls describes his theory as contractarian: 'my aim is to present a conception of justice which generalizes and carries to a higher level of abstraction the familiar theory of the social contract as found, say, in Locke, Rousseau, and Kant' (Rawls 1972: 11). The contract was a device for justifying obedience to the state, where the 'state' is understood as a coercive entity. Although details vary between the thinkers, there is common to all contract theories a three-part structure: a description of an initial situation in which there is no state (this is usually termed the state of nature); the contract itself, where the contract may be an actual historical act or, more plausibly, a hypothetical procedure; and finally, an outline of the political institutions – centred around the coercive state – into which people have contracted. Although the first great contract theorist was Thomas Hobbes, interestingly Rawls deliberately omits Hobbes from the above quoted list of political thinkers, arguing that 'for all its greatness, Hobbes's *Leviathan* raises special problems' (Rawls 1972: 11*n*). However, reflection on these problems provides a useful way into understanding Rawls's aims.

The prisoner's dilemma

Hobbes's *Leviathan* can be interpreted as an attempt to solve the prisoner's dilemma. The prisoner's dilemma is an imaginary 'game' intended to represent political relationships. We envisage two people arrested for a crime and interrogated separately. If both remain silent each will be convicted of a relatively minor offence, and spend a year in prison. If both confess, each will receive five years for a more serious offence. If one confesses but the other remains silent, the confessor will go free, while the other will receive a ten-year sentence. Clearly, the actions of one affect the outcome for the other, as can be seen from the pay-off table (the two numbers in each pair represent the years in prison for the first and second prisoners respectively):

Version 1		Second prisoner	
		Remains silent	Confesses
First prisoner	Remains silent	1, 1	10, 0
	Confesses	0, 10	5, 5

If we assume the prisoners are purely self-interested then each will attempt to achieve his first preference. It is useful to set out

the preference-ordering of the first prisoner and the consequence
for the second prisoner of each of the former's preferences:

	1st preference	2nd preference	3rd preference	4th preference
First prisoner	0, 10	1, 1	5, 5	10, 0
Second prisoner	10, 0	1, 1	5, 5	0, 10

It is not rational to remain silent while the other prisoner confesses,
so the likely outcome is that each will confess, with the consequence that each satisfies only his third preference. What makes
the game interesting is that each could do better by agreeing to
remain silent. The prisoner's dilemma is a non-zero sum game:
a gain for one prisoner does not result in an equivalent loss for
the other. The explanation of how, through co-operation, each
prisoner might move from his third to his second preference
is a contemporary rendition of the reasoning behind Hobbes's
contract theory. The third preference represents the non-
co-operation characteristic of the state of nature, the agreement
to remain silent is equivalent to the contract itself, and the satisfaction of the second preference equates to life under a state. Using
Rawls's terms, there are *burdens* as well as *benefits* to submitting to
a state – we are required to conform to laws that may, through
taxation, require us to hand over material resources, and will
in many different ways restrict our freedom. But we gain the
benefits of security, and with security comes increased prosperity and a guarantee that we will enjoy a significant amount of
personal freedom.

Some commentators argue the rational strategy for each
prisoner is to forgo his first preference in order to achieve his
second preference. This is incorrect: for each prisoner achieving his first preference should remain his goal. What he wants

is an agreement with the other prisoner that each will remain silent, but then to break the agreement in the hope that the other prisoner will honour it. Individual rationality dictates he should free-ride on the other's compliance – that is, gain the benefits of co-operation, which is the avoidance of four years (five less one) in prison, without paying the cost of co-operation, which is one year in prison. Of course, as rational actors each prisoner understands the motivations of the other, and so a voluntary agreement is ineffective. What they need is a third-party enforcer of the agreement. The enforcer imposes sanctions on free-riders, such that there is an incentive to comply. If each can be *assured* of the enforcer's effectiveness then a move from each prisoner's third preference to his second preference can be achieved. In political terms, the enforcer is the state.

Rawls accepts the existence of prisoner's dilemma-type situations, and of the logic of submission to the state as a resolution to it (Rawls 1972: 269–70). However, he raises – implicitly – three objections to Hobbes's argument. First, the existence of an enforcer, or state, does not fundamentally alter the motivations of those subject to it: each still seeks to satisfy his own interests. This engenders a fundamental instability in the political order: you are always looking over your shoulder at other people, convinced that given the opportunity they will break the law. Such law-breaking might, for example, take the form of evading payment of taxes necessary to maintain a police force. It would be better if people sometimes – indeed, mostly – acted in the interests of other people, that is if they were both *rational* – self-interested – but also *reasonable*, and so prepared to accept constraints on the pursuit of their self-interest. For Rawls, principles of justice are *necessary* because people are rational, but *possible* because they are also reasonable (Rawls 1972: 4).

The second objection to Hobbes can be broadened out into a critique of the aims of classical contract theory. Hobbes, Locke, Rousseau and Kant were preoccupied with the question of an individual's obligation to obey the state and its laws. A law by its nature commands obedience, but political obligation is concerned with the existence of moral reasons for obeying the law: by asking whether a person has a political obligation we put into question the legitimacy of law. From the preceding discussion it is not difficult to see how a contractarian might argue for political obligation. We are all better off under a state than in a state of nature and therefore we are under an obligation to obey the state. While Rawls does not reject the claim that we are better off under a state, this represents merely the starting point for a theory of justice. It is only a starting point because the benefits of co-operation might be unequally distributed. While in the above presentation of the prisoner's dilemma the benefits of an agreement to remain silent were equally distributed, without changing the structure of the dilemma we can consider a second version in which the gains from co-operation are unequally distributed:

| Version 2 | | Second prisoner | |
		Remains silent	**Confesses**
	Remains silent	4, 1	10, 0
First prisoner	**Confesses**	0, 10	6, 5

The preference-ordering of each prisoner is identical to the first example. The difference lies in the respective pay-offs from co-operation relative to non-co-operation: the first prisoner gains two years of freedom whereas the second prisoner gains four. It might therefore be *rational* for each prisoner to submit to an enforced agreement, but it is not necessarily *reasonable*. And this brings us to the third objection to Hobbes. In both examples there was a unique solution to the dilemma, but what if instead of one set of pay-offs there were multiple sets? Let us imagine that the agreement is not about confessing, or not, to a crime, but is concerned with the creation of political principles or institutions. We have to decide on the economic and political structure of society: should power be concentrated or dispersed? Should there be strong private property rights or, alternatively, collective ownership of economic resources? How much freedom should individuals have? Do we want an extensive welfare state or should individuals be required to buy health cover and education? Whatever is chosen, we are all better off under some kind of state than no state, but there is not a unique solution. The principles or institutions we choose will benefit people in different ways: if *a* represents the state of nature, and *b–z* a range of alternative political systems, then I am better off under any of *b–z* than under *a*, but my preferred system may not be shared by all other citizens.

The existence of moral motivations may exacerbate political conflict. In the absence of moral motivation those groups disadvantaged by the choice of a particular type of political structure – say, one based on strong private property rights – would not have much respect for the state, but they could not feel *resentment* at their situation, for resentment entails a belief that the rules are unfair. A sense of unfairness is a more significant source of political instability than the recognition that the political system simply works against one's self-interest. If there is a broad consensus that a particular form of political organization is unfair, and an historic example would be racial segregation in the Deep South of the USA, then a resolution is possible, albeit after a period of instability. More difficult is a situation in which the claims of a particular group are not widely recognized. For example, many people believe that an unequal distribution of wealth is legitimate, for it reflects the unequal distribution of natural ability, and differing propensities to hard work: those who make money deserve to keep it, though possibly subject to guaranteeing a minimum level of welfare for all. Likewise, there may be considerable disagreement about how much freedom individuals should enjoy. The apparent absence of a consensus over the fair distribution of wealth, freedom and other goods poses a challenge to the stability of the political system.

The original position

Rawls aims to resolve these disputes. Along with classical contract theorists he accepts the logic of the state, but the key issue is not about obedience to the state but about how we stabilize a political order on the basis of agreement to the fair distribution of freedom, power and material resources. And as I suggested at the beginning of the chapter there are two dimensions to his work: method and substance. His method presupposes a distinction between the rational and the reasonable. Pure rationality involves simply assessing a particular political system from one's own standpoint: what do I get out of this system compared with any alternative? Reasonableness requires viewing a political system from the standpoint of each person who will be affected by it. I have to put myself in the shoes of another person and ask myself if I were that person would I agree to this system rather than some alternative. Rawls sets up a thought-experiment: we are to assess alternative conceptions of justice from what he terms the original position. The most important feature of the original position is the denial of knowledge of your identity – you choose principles of justice without knowing what position you occupy in society. Indeed, you do not know even your particular society.

While the 'veil of ignorance' is its most memorable aspect, the original position has two other important components: primary goods and motivational assumptions. Furthermore, the original position is a device of representation, meaning that agents in the original position represent agents outside it in the real world. In fact, if you are in the original position then the person you represent is yourself under a different description. Human beings,

Rawls argues, are capable of acting morally, where morality is defined as the capacity to be moved by another person's interests, and the original position is intended to capture this idea. If you do not know your age, sex, values and so on, you are forced to put yourself in the shoes of each other person and see the world from his or her perspective.

If you are denied knowledge of your ends – that is, those things which you seek to protect or advance or achieve, such as a particular career, relationships with identifiable family and friends or a set of beliefs about the world – then you need some substitute ends. Given we do not know our identities, these ends must be shared by all agents in the original position, and they must be of fundamental importance. Rawls argues that each person desires to maximize his or her share of the (social) primary goods, which are rights and liberties, powers and opportunities, income and wealth, and the bases of self-respect. These goods are all-purpose means to the realization of a multiplicity of different ends. There is an objection to this argument: the primary goods are not equally valued by all people. A hedonist will require a higher share of the goods than an ascetic. To deal with this problem, the primary goods must not be of purely instrumental value: while the ascetic may require fewer primary goods than the hedonist, both must be capable of imagining being the other, such that while they may not *use* the same amount of primary goods, they recognize it is rational to *have available* the same amount.

The third important aspect of the original position is a set of motivational assumptions. These assumptions are advanced for the purposes of generating principles of justice and are not a description of how real people behave. As well as seeking to maximize his share of the primary goods, an agent is non-envious, disinterested and willing to live by principles he has chosen. The reasoning behind these assumptions is explained in Chapter 3, but a general point can be made here. There is a split between the rational and reasonable: rationality entails the successful pursuit of your own interests, whereas reasonableness involves a willingness to see the world from the perspective of another person and act accordingly. Agents in the original position are directly rational and only indirectly reasonable: they are rational insofar as they seek to maximize their own share of the primary goods, but reasonable in that they are willing, and know that other agents are willing, to live by whatever principles are chosen. Some critics of Rawls argue that his theory combines the contradictory impulses of self-interest and morality, but this is a misunderstanding. Rawls makes an analytical distinction between self-interest and morality precisely to motivate people to act morally. Agents in the original position have a formal sense of justice, meaning that they are willing to live by whatever principles of justice are chosen. This contrasts with a substantive moral sense that certain principles are valid. To be motivated people must see principles of justice as a product of *their choice*, but to give substance to principles they need some idea of what interests people have.

A focus on the veil of ignorance to the exclusion of the other elements of the original position will result in a distorted picture of Rawls's theory of justice. Certainly, the idea of the veil makes for a useful intellectual exercise in which people are asked to imagine they do not know their sex, class, sexual orientation and so on, and are then given the task of choosing principles of justice. Even if they do not choose Rawls's two principles of justice they may well opt for principles more egalitarian than they would choose under conditions of full self-knowledge. But the results of this exercise, while interesting, may not be particularly informative, for the aim of Rawls's theory is to select principles that will operate in the real world. The test of the validity of his method is whether *over time* the chosen principles can become embedded in the culture of a society. For this reason, much of Rawls's work – including at least a third of *A Theory of Justice* – is concerned with the 'stability' of the principles, meaning the possible operation of the principles in a world where we do know our identities.

Principles of justice

If procedures validate outcomes, that is, principles are just because they would be *chosen* under fair conditions, then in the original position we must be free to propose *any* principles. Many proposals will be rejected because of the formal requirements of justice. For example, one such requirement is that any principle must be public. If I were to propose that society be run on the basis of secret principles, or principles that could not by their nature be public – such as the 'will of the ruler is the source of all law' – then the proposal would be rejected as formally invalid. Other principles are not formally invalid, but would lead to social conflict: the principle that 'each person should pursue his own interests as he sees fit' could not be put into operation. Once we have eliminated formally invalid and unstable principles, we are left with a range of serious candidates for adoption: various versions of utilitarianism, perfectionism, intuitionism and what Rawls calls the democratic conception.

Rawls's theory of justice is both ambitious and modest, and this combination of ambition and modesty is most apparent in his argument for what he terms the 'two principles of justice'. The precise formulation of the two principles is set out on pages 52–3, but in summary the first principle guarantees each person an equal set of liberties, while the second ensures a certain level of material resources – it requires that each person be as well off as possible. The two principles are lexically ordered, meaning the first must be fully satisfied before enacting the second. But these two principles are a particular (special conception) version of a general principle (general conception). The general conception requires that inequalities work to the advantage of the worst-off. Rawls invites the reader to endorse the general conception but does so through setting out a particular version of it, namely, the two principles. Of course, Rawls believes the two principles represent the best, or most coherent, version but he leaves open the possibility that there be might be a superior version of the general conception. If the reader is persuaded that the method of choosing principles of justice is valid, and that the general conception is preferable to the alternatives, then Rawls's book could be deemed a success.

The difficulty is that many critics, even those who accept Rawls's method, argue that the democratic conception is not the most likely outcome of rational deliberation in the original position. The most credible option is average utilitarianism with a floor. Simplifying somewhat at this stage, a principle of average utility entails maximizing the average level of utility with the proviso that the worst-off have a minimum level of resources, where the minimum might be an absolute amount, or more plausibly, a fraction of the average. While this is not an argument in favour of agents *behind a veil of ignorance* selecting average utility with a floor, observations of real liberal-democratic societies suggest that most people endorse this principle: citizens want economic growth and increasing personal income, but also support a safety net for the poorest. The motivations for supporting such a policy may be diverse: fear that you could end up in the poorest class; concern about the crime and social disorder that poverty might engender; genuine sympathy with the suffering of the poor combined with recognition of the need for incentives. Obviously, Rawls is working with a moral construction procedure that may throw up principles at variance with everyday beliefs, and that seeks to change those beliefs. Nonetheless, experimental approaches to the selection of principles has produced results in line with everyday attitudes, and so Rawls has his work cut out persuading us that the general conception – priority to the worst-off – would be endorsed from a standpoint of moral equality.

In the next two chapters I outline in more detail Rawls's method for choosing principles of justice (Chapter 3) and discuss the two principles of justice and the main competitors (Chapter 4). Chapters 5 and 6 subject both the principles, especially the difference principle (Chapter 5), and the method for choosing principles (Chapter 6), to closer scrutiny and criticism. Chapter 7 rounds off the discussion of Rawls's *A Theory of Justice* (and earlier work), with a consideration of two issues in what he calls non-ideal (or 'partial compliance) theory: civil disobedience and punishment. In the last two chapters I consider Rawls's later work, which includes what I regard as a significant revision of the method of justification, and his reflections on international relations, in *The Law of Peoples*.

Further reading

General orientations to Rawls's work can be found in Kukathas and Pettit (1990), Chapter 1. Thomas Nagel in Freeman (2003) is also useful. See also Kukathas (2003; vol. 1), part 1, and Kukathas (2003; vol. 2), part 1.

3

The original position

The gist of Rawls's argument is that just principles are those which would be chosen in a situation in which agents are free and equal. People should be motivated to respect principles which they recognize they have chosen, or would choose, under the hypothetical conditions of the original position. The original position is characterized not only by the freedom to choose moral principles, but also by equality between agents. Indeed, freedom and equality are intimately related: if there is an unequal relationship, such as exists in the second version of the prisoner's dilemma, then those who are relatively disadvantaged do not enjoy the same degree of freedom as the relatively advantaged. As Rawls observes: 'to each according to his threat advantage is not a conception of justice' (Rawls 1972: 134).

The validity of principles derives from the *procedure* by which they are chosen rather than because they accord with a pre-existing set of moral values. The full philosophical significance of the idea of choosing (rather than discovering) principles of justice will become clearer in later chapters, but the key point here is that if choice is taken seriously, then the method by which principles of justice are selected must be detached from what Rawls believes rational agents will, in fact, choose. It is completely open to agents to propose any principles. Although Rawls suggests they will converge on a general conception of justice – namely, priority to the worst-off – of which the two principles together constitute a special conception, a distinction must be drawn between the method whereby principles of justice are selected, and what is chosen. Consequently, the next four chapters are organized around the distinction between method and substance, with this chapter and Chapter 6 focused on method, and Chapters 4 and 5 on the principles Rawls believes agents would choose.

Parameters of the theory

Rawls's theory of justice is political in that it is restricted to a particular sphere of society. Many moral questions fall outside the scope of the theory, and it is therefore important to map out the parameters of the theory. First, the theory applies to the basic structure of society and not to all social relations. Second, Rawls is concerned with domestic rather than international justice, meaning that the primary moral relationship is between the individual citizen and the state, and by extension relationships between citizens through state structures. Third, in selecting principles of justice agents assume they live in a well-ordered society, that is, a society in which citizens (strictly) comply with the chosen principles, so that while the theory has practical implications for the real world, there are limits on the application of the principles to issues of public policy. Some political issues, such as punishment and civil disobedience, arise because there is less than strict compliance. Fourth, relations between human beings are governed by principles of justice, and no attempt is made to explain the moral relationship between humankind and the non-human world. We start with the basic structure argument.

How well a person's life goes depends on a number of factors or 'contingencies': social class background, natural ability and good or bad fortune (Rawls 2001: 55). While the organization of society has a direct impact on social class – because the state can be empowered to redistribute wealth and other goods – it also determines the *consequences* of the exploitation of natural ability and fortune. The area of social life in which state activity has a significant impact Rawls terms the 'basic structure of society' and this, he argues, is the main concern – or primary subject – of justice (Rawls 1972: 7). He gives as examples of institutions within the basic structure the legal protection of freedom of thought and conscience, competitive markets, private property and the family.

The basic structure argument has important implications for Rawls's theory. First, while inequality calls for principles of justice, inequality is not the only problem human beings face. Other problems include how to coordinate activity, ensure efficiency and guarantee the stability of institutions. A theory of justice *directly* addresses the problem of inequality, but *indirectly* it must be concerned with these other problems. Second, even when we are focused on the question of justice, principles of justice – understood as coercively enforced principles – do not exhaust all aspects of justice. Rawls draws a distinction between the justice *of* the basic structure, and justice *within* the basic structure. Take as an example the family. In addition to genetic advantages passed on from (biological) parents to children such things as the number of books in the family home, the quality of conversation between parents and children, the range of leisure activities and diet will affect the intellectual development of children. In choosing principles of justice we can allow these factors to determine the distribution of educational achievement, and, by extension, income and other goods, or attempt to 'nullify' them through distributing extra educational resources to children disadvantaged by their inheritance and upbringing. While it is open to agents in the original position to choose whatever principles they wish, we can assume it is legitimate to regard educational opportunity as an appropriate good for distribution, and to this extent the family is an institution within the basic structure of society.

The justice *of* the family must, however, be distinguished from justice *within* the family. Household labour and child-rearing responsibilities, as well as income, are distributed within families as well as between families. Furthermore, there has developed an ideal of the family as held together by ties of sentiment (or affection) rather than the imperatives of material reproduction. While this may be a normative ideal it nonetheless conditions attitudes to the relationship of the family to the state. This difference is significant in at least two ways: it may not be possible to redistribute affection in the same manner as income or freedom and even if it were possible it would not be *desirable* to attempt a redistribution. We can summarize the basic structure argument in this way: a theory of justice is a moral theory but one limited to the basic structure of society, so that while we have a moral duty to respect principles of justice, morality consists of much more, such as special duties to family and friends.

The second major limitation is that principles of justice apply to relations between citizens in a self-contained – closed – society and not to the relations between societies, or states. Rawls clarifies the subject of social justice by distinguishing three levels of justice – local, domestic and global – and maintaining that social justice applies to the domestic level. Local justice has been illustrated by the issue of the distribution of resources within a family; other examples include the rules governing voluntary associations, such as clubs or churches. As domestic justice only *indirectly* affects local justice, so it is with global justice, or what Rawls terms the law of peoples. In this regard Rawls adopts a traditional approach to political theory: the primary ethical relationship holds between the individual and the state. And issues in international relations – military intervention, global distributive justice, human rights – are only of indirect concern for individuals. It is interesting that Rawls's stated reason for writing his last significant work, *The Law of Peoples*, is to establish whether or not liberal democracies should tolerate non-liberal societies, and, by extension, whether individual citizens of a liberal democracy have an obligation to support military intervention by their state in the affairs of another state.

The assumption that principles of justice are operative in a self-contained, closed society should not be understood as an endorsement of the *nation* as intrinsically valuable. The principles of justice will necessarily be coercively enforced, and that presupposes the existence of a *state* which we are obliged to obey. But the state is a juridical and not a cultural concept. The assumption of a closed society is introduced in order to block off an argument for obligation to the state attributed – in Rawls's view, unfairly – to Locke, namely that an individual is expressing consent – *tacit consent* – to the existing social institutions by remaining in a particular territory and using its resources (Rawls 1972: 112; Locke 1992: 348). For Rawls, leaving the society in which one was born is such a serious step that deciding not to leave cannot reasonably be interpreted as constituting consent. That is not to say that there would not be among the principles of justice a right to emigrate, but rather we cannot assume that the possibility of emigration somehow validates unjust laws.

The third important background aspect to Rawls's theory is the assumption that principles of justice are to be selected for a well-ordered society. A society is well-ordered when it is 'not only designed to advance the good of its members but when it is also effectively regulated by a public conception of justice' (Rawls 1972: 5). That means: (a) everybody accepts and knows that the others accept the same principles of justice, and (b) the institutions of the basic structure generally satisfy and are generally known to satisfy these principles. The double-headed nature of both (a) and (b) is important: following the logic of the resolution of the prisoner's dilemma it is essential that we not only live by principles of justice but are *seen* to live by them. At the risk of a proliferation of concepts, Rawls's assumption of a well-ordered society spawns two further concepts, or pairs of concepts: partial and strict compliance, and ideal and non-ideal theory. The distinction between the two pairs of concepts is not of great significance at this stage – 'compliance' focuses on the individual, and his or her behaviour, whereas the latter pair denotes a type of theory.

Much of political theory addresses situations of partial compliance. For example, how do we deal with law-breaking? We need a theory of punishment. What is the morally correct response to human rights violations? We require a theory of humanitarian intervention. Rawls does not deny the importance of these issues, and indeed accepts they are at the heart of every-day politics, but argues that a systematic grasp of ideal theory is necessary as a preliminary to dealing with the 'more press-ing problems' of non–ideal theory (Rawls 1972: 9). The one part of *A Theory of Justice* concerned with partial compliance is his discussion of civil disobedience (Rawls 1972: 363–91). Such a discussion is necessary because agents in the original position will likely endorse majority voting as a means of settling political disputes, but majority rule has to be rendered compatible with respect for individual rights. Civil disobedience is made concep-tually possible by the requirement to reconcile majority rule and minority rights where the two conflict. Elsewhere is in his work Rawls discusses other issues falling under 'non-compliance'. An influential early essay, 'Two Concepts of Rules', deals, in part, with the justification of punishment, and *The Law of Peoples*, while primarily concerned with ideal international justice also addresses relations between well-ordered societies (which need not be liberal) and what he calls outlaw states and 'burdened' societies.

Finally, Rawls argues that his theory cannot settle all moral questions, but rather the task is to focus on a particular moral relationship between human beings, namely, how they distrib-ute those resources which fundamentally affect their lives. As suggested above, there are many other moral issues that arise in society, but in addition there are also relations between human beings and non-human animals, and between humanity and nature in the widest sense. Rawls does not reject the relationship of humanity to nature as unimportant, but argues that we need first to settle questions of justice before testing the compatibility of a theory of justice with other possible moral principles, such as respect for the earth (Rawls 1972: 17). Ecologists are unlikely to be satisfied with Rawls's approach, maintaining that the idea of morality as the product of human choice is incompatible with an ecocentric ethic.

Motivation

As I argued in Chapter 2, the key feature of the original position is the veil of ignorance. This controls what information is available to agents in the original position: they are denied knowledge of their individual identities, but possess general knowledge of society, which includes awareness that they live in a society characterized by a *moderate* scarcity of resources. Each also knows he or she represents somebody in the real world. Rawls attributes to people in the original position a certain psychology, or set of motivations. He makes these assumptions for the purposes of his theory, and does not claim that real people possess this psychology. Human beings are agents – they *desire* (have preferences for) certain things. Everyday observation of human behaviour reveals that people differ significantly in what they desire: think of career aspirations, or recreational pursuits or sexual preferences. Denial of self-knowledge, as required by the veil, means agents no longer experience or have access to their particular desires and preferences. To pursue our interests in ignorance of our particular preferences requires focusing on the general, or all purpose, means to the satisfaction of preferences.

All rational agents are assumed to want social primary goods. The social primary goods are rights and liberties, powers and opportunities, income and wealth, and the bases of self-respect (Rawls 1972: 62). These are valuable for many different ends. If, for example, you choose a career trading in stocks and shares, you need the freedom and material resources to train for, and pursue, such a career. Likewise, if you opt for life in an apparently self-sufficient community on a remote island you will also need freedom, opportunities and income. The ends – being a stockbroker, living on a remote island – are clearly different, but the means are common. The primary goods play a central role in Rawls's theory: we cannot *directly* promote our interests, because we do not know our particular desires or preferences – career plans, recreational interests, sexual desires and so on – but we can seek to maximize the *opportunities* for satisfying our preferences.

Rawls has been challenged on his claim that each person attaches equal value to the primary goods. To live in a self-sufficient community certainly does require primary goods – after all, Robinson Crusoe had to acquire the skills to survive on his desert island – but it may require significantly fewer than that needed for other lifestyles. In a later series of lectures, Rawls argued the primary goods – especially freedom – enable us to achieve our ends in a certain way (Rawls 1999b: 312). Simply stated, freedom adds something: for example, a marriage freely entered into has a quality absent from one which is arranged, even when under the two scenarios – freely chosen and arranged – the same two people marry. It follows that freedom is a constituent part of the ends we pursue.

The second motivational claim has already been stated, but requires some elaboration: agents in the original position seek to maximize their share of the primary goods. Such a motivation would appear at first sight incompatible with the impartiality that is imposed on agents by the veil of ignorance. Some critics have argued that Rawls's theory oscillates uncomfortably between morality and self-interest (Barry 1989: 241–54). But this is to misunderstand the role the original position plays in Rawls's theory: how we behave in the original position is not a full description of how real human beings behave in a well-ordered society. Rawls distinguishes the rational and the reasonable. In everyday language, this distinction can be understood in the comment made about a selfish person: 'given his interests his actions are *rational*, but not *reasonable*'. In the original position the agent is constrained by the veil of ignorance, so he does not know his particular interests, but is motivated to maximize his absolute level of primary goods, which are the means through which he pursues his particular interests. Consequently, the agent is directly rational but indirectly reasonable. The only way the agent could be directly reasonable would be if he came into the original position with a substantive set of moral beliefs, which motivated him to act. But acting on such beliefs would undermine the idea of the original position as a choice situation: we need to enter it without prejudice to a pre-existing morality. Agents *are* moral in that they seek agreement on moral principles, and – most importantly – are motivated to respect whatever principles are chosen, but this 'formal' moral sense is distinct from any substantive moral sense, that is, any commitment to *particular* moral principles. By isolating the rational from the reasonable we generate content for the principles of justice. In the original position agents are *rationally autonomous*, meaning they understand their own interests and know how to advance them, but outside the original position, in a well-ordered society governed by principles of justice, human beings are *fully autonomous*. In full autonomy the rational is incorporated in, but subordinated to, the reasonable. It follows that people in the original position take the choice of principles very seriously, knowing that those they represent in the real world will feel what Rawls calls the 'strains of commitment' to the chosen principles (Rawls 1972: 145).

Two further features of motivation in the original position flow from the distinction between rationality and reasonableness. Agents are mutually disinterested and non-envious. It is important to stress once again that Rawls makes these assumptions for the purpose of generating principles of justice. He is not claiming real human beings are not envious, or even less that they take no interest in other people's welfare. The effect of assuming mutual disinterest is that *agents in the original position* concern themselves only with their own welfare, and not with the welfare of identifiable family and friends. Arguably, Rawls's assertion of mutual disinterest is rendered redundant by the veil of ignorance: we do not know who we are and therefore we cannot know the identities of our families and friends. However, it may be that Rawls seeks to rule out the possibility that agent-relativity will affect the chosen principles. Something is agent-relative if the identity of the agent is taken to be morally relevant. Even behind the veil we might conceivably propose a principle that 'parents should always give priority to *their* children over other children', even though we do not know the identities of our children, or if we have children. We could not agree to this principle because the moral right to give absolute priority to your children lacks compossibility – that is, parents will be brought into irreconcilable conflict with one another.

Envy, more so than ties of affection, undermines any agreement. Envious people assess the value of their own resources by comparing them to those of other people. Were agents in the original position envious the overall level of resources might be considerably less, as agents bid each other down to avoid differentials in the distribution of resources. By assuming agents have a 'secure sense of their own worth' and so are not envious, the chosen principles of justice should work to the advantage of all (Rawls 1972: 144). Once the veil is lifted and principles are operative in a society of real people we can assess whether envy is a problem. If it proves a problem, then principles selected under the non-envy condition would be unstable, and we would be forced to revise them.

Proceduralism

We now have in place an outline of what motivates agents in the original position. It is useful to step back from the details of the original position and reflect on what kind of moral or political theory Rawls is advancing. At the core of the theory is the idea that procedures validate outcomes, and consequently choice plays a fundamental role in explaining why we are morally bound to a set of political principles. Such a theory can be labelled 'constructivist'. Constructivism has the advantage over alternative methods of justification that the chosen principles can be recognized by agents as (at least, hypothetically) the product of their own actions (choice), and therefore they are more likely to be motivated to respect them. But it also generates challenges, chief of which is explaining the moral objectivity of the chosen principles: if we can choose then why not choose anything at all? And if we choose the same principles, then in what sense is it really a choice?

Rawls distinguishes three procedures, or forms of procedural justice: perfect, imperfect and pure. The first he illustrates with the division of a cake; a fair division will result if it is agreed in advance that the person who cuts the cake takes the last piece (Rawls 1972: 85). The procedure guarantees − perfects − an independently existing criterion of justice, namely, that of equality. In contrast, a procedure is imperfect if there is no such guarantee, an example being a criminal trial, in which the criterion of justice is the conviction of the guilty and the acquittal of the innocent as a result of a search for the truth (Rawls 1972: 85−6). The original position is a representation of *pure procedural justice*, for there is no criterion of justice independent of the choices that agents make (Rawls 1972: 120). Rather, it is the procedure itself that validates what is chosen, and for this reason Rawls characterizes his theory as one in which the right is prior to the good (Rawls 1972: 451).

Rawls follows Kant against utilitarian and perfectionist theories which, it is claimed, give priority to the good over the right. These theories Rawls terms teleological, because they posit an end – *telos* – which we should pursue. The formulation of this distinction and of the corresponding relationships is attributed to British philosopher W. D. Ross, who defined the good as 'that which is worth pursuing' and the right as 'that which is obligatory' (Ross 1998: 3). Put another way, rightness is a quality of *action* and goodness a quality of the *ends* we pursue, where an end might be something relatively concrete like the appreciation of opera, sporting excellence or religious observance, or, alternatively, something more general such as the maximization of pleasure or preference-satisfaction. The best way to understand the relationship between the right and the good is to think what motivates the agent: does he respect principles of justice because he (hypothetically) chose them (right is prior to the good), or because those ends have intrinsic value (good is prior to the right)? It may be argued that choice cannot generate validity: if the choice-situation (original position) is fair then it is fair against a set of unchosen background conditions, so validity is derived from the conditions under which the choice is made, and not the act of choice itself. Put simply, agents in the original position are forced to be moral by the veil of ignorance, but they did not choose to go behind the veil. On the other hand, if agents choose with knowledge of their own identities they will not reach agreement, for, as suggested by the second version of the prisoner's dilemma, there is no outcome which maximizes the respective positions of all agents.

One way out of this bind is to identify rightness not with a particular choice but with the *capacity* for choice. This changes the source of validity from an individual act to a description of the kind of person capable of making a contract. We then say that political institutions are valid if they could be the product of a contract, where the contracting parties are the kind of people capable of entering into contracts and the conditions under which any hypothetical choice is made models their equal freedom, or autonomy. Rightness is prior to goodness in that the conditions under which the principles of justice are chosen reflect the idea of agents as autonomous. We need, however, to distinguish two types of condition, formal and substantive. Rawls argues that principles of justice possess formal features, and although he does not make it explicit, these qualities are connected to the idea of human beings as responsible agents. The substantive features build on the formal features.

Rawls lists five formal features of principles of justice, meaning characteristics which any principle must have. These are generality, universality, publicity, ordering and finality:

- **Generality** precludes the use of proper names or 'rigged definitive descriptions' (Rawls 1972: 131).
- **Universality** means principles must apply to everyone.
- **Publicity** holds that a principle must be transparent to all those who are bound by it.
- **Ordering** entails, among other things, transitivity; that is, if principle A is preferred to principle B, and B to C, then C cannot be preferred to A.
- **Finality** involves the recognition of principles of justice as the 'final court of appeal' in practical reasoning (Rawls 1972: 135).

The appeal to formal right provides part of an answer to the standard criticism of contractarianism identified earlier: if agents are free to choose then surely they can choose any 'principles', however intuitively immoral? The response is to say that agents choose, but what generates validity is not a particular choice, but the process of choosing, and that process is constrained by the five formal features. To generate a full conception of justice requires supplementing the formal features of justice with certain substantive features of human agency, features which do not follow from the concept of a principle and these include the idea of an agent possessing the moral powers of rationality and reasonableness discussed in the last section.

Reflective equilibrium and stability

Despite Rawls's emphasis on choosing or constructing principles of justice, he relies on two concepts which appear to undermine the construction procedure: *reflective equilibrium* and *stability*. Rawls argues that certain moral beliefs, such as the belief that religious intolerance is wrong, function as 'fixed points' against which the chosen principles are to be assessed (Rawls 1972: 19–20). If the principles are not compatible with those beliefs then we must go back and alter them until chosen principles and fixed points are in reflective equilibrium. At first sight this appears to undermine the idea of constructing principles of justice, which entails the validity of principles deriving from their being the product of a procedure rather than conforming to values simply given to us. Furthermore, if the choice made in the original position is a 'one-off' then how can we go back and alter it?

The idea of reflective equilibrium is, in fact, compatible with construction. For Rawls the aim of political philosophy is to 'articulate and to make explicit those shared notions and principles thought to be latent in common sense' (Rawls 1999b: 306). Political philosophy addresses itself to practical rather than epistemological questions: we *choose* principles of justice rather than *discover* an independently existing moral order. The construction procedure is intended to 'model' the practical, or volitional, nature of morality, while reflective equilibrium aims to reconcile the volitional with our everyday intuitions.

Like Kant, to whom he owes a great deal, Rawls assumes that ordinary people are capable of being rational and reasonable. The task of a theory of justice is not so much to instruct people in questions of justice but to reassure ourselves that our everyday beliefs are not erroneous. Of course, we do not live in a just society, and political philosophy must be critical, but the crucial point is that we can, without contradiction, appeal to common-sense moral beliefs or 'intuitions' and at the same time conceive of political principles as the product of a hypothetical choice procedure, for the choice-procedure is a way of bringing out the underlying rationality and reasonableness of everyday belief. Rawls's insistence on the duality of intuition and construction derives from a concern with motivation: a tight connection is drawn between the recognition of principles of justice and action. I am motivated to act on principles I recognize *could* be the product of my choice.

Many interpreters stress Rawls's coherentist epistemology, which is contrasted with 'foundationalism'. Foundationalism carries the metaphorical implication of a building with foundations of non-inferential belief – beliefs not derived, or inferred, from other beliefs. It thus privileges certain beliefs or claims, from which others are derived, just as the walls, floors and roof of a building rest on the foundations. Coherentism, on the other hand, does not privilege any particular beliefs, but rather beliefs are mutually supportive. If we interpret Rawls's theory as coherentist, the original position is not the *foundation* of the principles, but is primarily a method for exploring everyday intuitions about justice, and ensuring they fit together. It follows that the outcome of the choice in the original position must be tested against strongly held everyday beliefs until outcome and beliefs are in equilibrium. It is, however, important to distinguish two versions of coherentism. In the first, everyday moral intuitions are simply the beliefs of 'our society', while in the second coherence is achieved through employing principles of reason which transcend the particular beliefs of our society. These principles of reason are not the foundations of our political principles, but rather the necessary conditions for any valid moral principles. The formal features of principles of justice, discussed in the last section, exemplify such principles of reason.

Any apparent tension between agents in the original position recognizing they have only one choice, and the possibility of revising those principles if they are incompatible with their considered judgements about right and wrong is dissolved once we recognize the original position is a thought experiment, and that rational agency in the original position is an abstraction from full agency. Rawls talks of three perspectives: of you and me as political thinkers; of agents in the original position; and of citizens living under principles of justice (Rawls 1999b: 320–1). It is political thinkers who engage in reflective equilibrium, whereas it is agents in the original position who have only one chance to choose principles of justice. Mention of the third perspective – of citizens – brings us to the other concept which appears in tension with the idea of construction: stability. Agents in the original position choose principles knowing that once the veil has been lifted they will be aware of their identities and yet still recognize the moral force of the chosen principles. Outside the original position we need to be assured that other people will comply with the chosen principles. If there are tendencies towards injustice, and a sufficiently large number of people are moved to act unjustly, then society is unstable. Rawls argues that coercion is one way of ensuring stability, but a desire to live by principles is a stronger guarantor of stability (Rawls 1972: 497). It is for agents in the original position, with knowledge of sociology and psychology, to assess the likelihood that principles will be stable. Stability became a major concern for Rawls in his later work (Rawls 1996), where he defines the problem of stability as that of reaching agreement in a society marked by an 'ineliminable pluralism' of conceptions of the good.

Further reading

Introductory and general discussions of Rawls's method for justifying principles of justice include Barry (1973), Chapters 1–4; Kukathas and Pettit (1990), Chapter 2; Scanlon in Freeman (2003). Book-length critiques include Sandel (1998) and Robert Paul Wolff (1977). Parts 1 and 2 of Daniels (1989) – on the original position and 'questions of method' – are useful, especially the essays by Nagel and Dworkin. On the primary goods and the rationality of agents in the original position, see the essays by Arrow, Buchanan and Sen in Richardson and Weithman (1999; vol. 1). For a discussion of Rawls's rejection of utilitarianism, read Lyons, Kavka and Barry in Richardson and Weithman (1999; vol. 3), and Scheffler in Freeman (2003). On perfectionism, see Nielsen in Richardson and Weithman (1999; vol. 3). Hare discusses reflective equilibrium in Richardson and Weithman (1999; vol. 2). Also, see Kukathas (2003; vol. 1), part 3 (original position), part 4 (reflective equilibrium), and Kukathas (2003; vol. 2), part 4 (primary goods).

4

Principles of justice

Agents in the original position are free to propose any principles they wish although, of course, they must achieve unanimous agreement. Given they are identically situated, the unanimity requirement is not onerous. However, determining what they would in fact choose is more challenging. Rawls claims they would choose the two principles of justice, but concedes that they might select different principles, hence the distinction between method and substance. Although there is no limit on what can be proposed, the menu of possible principles will be limited by the formal characteristics of a moral principle (discussed in the last section of Chapter 3). Other principles are ruled out as implausible or likely to be unstable. In this chapter I discuss in detail the two principles of justice. The concern is with both the internal coherence of the principles – whether these are compatible with one another – and the likelihood agents in the original position would choose them, rather than an alternative conception of justice.

Options

An agent in the original position is free to propose any principle(s) of justice. However, to simplify matters Rawls presents a menu of the most likely candidate principles (Rawls 1972: 124; I have altered the order):

1. Everyone acts fairly except me [free-riding].
2. Everyone serves my interests – I get what I want [first-person dictatorship].
3. Everyone is allowed to advance his interests as he wishes [general egoism].
4. We maximize the aggregate level of goods [classical utilitarianism].
5. Option 4 but with a minimum level of goods for each individual.
6. We maximize the average (per capita) level of goods [average utilitarianism].
7. Option 6 but with a minimum level of goods for each individual.
8. Certain ways of life are to be privileged because they have greater intrinsic value [perfectionism].
9. We balance a list of prima facie valid principles; for example, we make an intuitive judgement about the correct trade-off between freedom and equality should they conflict [intuitionism].
10. The two principles of justice [democratic conception].

Rawls argues that agents will choose option 10, although it is important to note that the two principles are a particular version (special conception) of the democratic conception (which is a general conception). He regards utilitarianism, and especially average utilitarianism (options 6 and 7) as providing the most credible alternative to the two principles (Rawls 1972: vii–viii). We start, however, with various forms of egoism (options 1–3), perfectionism (option 8) and intuitionism (option 9).

Strictly speaking the first three options are not moral conceptions. Free-riding (option 1) is ruled out by the strains of commitment: agents in the original position are prepared to live by the principles they have chosen and each knows the other is prepared to do so, therefore they could not choose to free-ride on others' compliance with the agreed principles. First-person dictatorship (option 2) is excluded by the generality requirement: principles of justice must not make reference to identifiable individuals, even if the agent in the original position does not know whether he will be the dictator. Since agents in the original position would be stupid to choose a principle such as 'Adolf Hitler's will is the source of all law', there may seem little point in discussing further the option of first-person dictatorship, but there is an interesting connection between the formal invalidity of that option and the veil of ignorance which precludes an agent taking the risk that he will not be Adolf Hitler. Since the veil denies agents knowledge of their identities the selection of a principle that identifies a particular agent is irrational: it amounts to the *arbitrary* selection of a person rather than a principle applicable to all agents. This reinforces the connection made in the last chapter between autonomous choice and moral objectivity: rationality coincides with the formal requirements of 'right' (see page 41).

Of the first group of principles we are left with universal egoism (option 3). This principle may violate the requirement of 'finality' – the endorsement of egoism would amount to the rejection of any moral principles, including individual rights. Were we to say that egoism requires me to respect your pursuit of your interests that would be contradictory, for not interfering in your actions entails a constraint on me. Universal egoism should not be confused with Rawls's claim that agents *inside* the original position pursue their own self-interest. As suggested in chapter 3, Rawls makes that assumption for the purposes of giving content to the principles of justice; the behaviour of agents in the original position is an abstraction from how they will behave outside it.

We now consider what are properly moral conceptions, starting with perfectionism. Rawls argues that perfectionism is a teleological theory which understands the good as 'the realization of human excellence in the various forms of culture' (Rawls 1972: 25). Duties are defined relative to standards of human excellence. What those duties actually require of individuals will depend on the nature of human excellence and the weight given to it. At one extreme is Nietzsche's emphasis on striving to produce great men, while at the other is a belief in a plurality of goods, which most, if not all, people are capable of pursuing (Rawls 1972: 325). A perfectionist conception of justice must hold some ways of life are intrinsically more valuable than others – they are worth pursuing whether or not large numbers of people desire them. Religious forms of life often embody perfectionist ideals, but there are secular versions. Agents denied knowledge of their conceptions of the good would, Rawls argues, not risk endorsing a perfectionist ideal for fear the chosen ideal would not be compatible with the conception of the good they in fact hold (Rawls 1972: 327–8). However, it may be argued that no coherent conception of justice can maintain that all ways of life are of equal value, and certainly the original position itself places value on the two moral powers (the rational and the reasonable), with the implication that human autonomy is intrinsically valuable, or more accurately, *constitutively* valuable. But insofar as holding freedom to be constitutively valuable implies a kind of perfectionism, such liberal perfectionism is distinct from non-liberal variants because agents are not required to pursue freedom; rather the justification of the political system makes appeal to the value of freedom. Liberal perfectionism does not coerce action, but must concede ways of life that embody freedom will be more successful in a liberal society than those which do not.

Consider now intuitionism, of which there are different forms. Eighteenth-century philosophers of the moral sense school argued that God implanted in human beings a sense of right and wrong. Later thinkers developed a non-theistic but still metaphysical intuitionism (Hudson 1967: 18–22). G. E. Moore argued that a moral belief entailed intuiting a non-natural property of an action. When we condemn an action as 'bad', or praise an action as 'good', the properties of goodness or badness are taken to be equivalent to colours, which are properties of mind imposed upon objects external to mind (Moore 1903: 7). Intuitionism is traditionally a *meta-ethical* theory, which explains the nature of morality, distinct from an *ethical* theory, and provides rules to follow or values to pursue. For that reason it can be combined with an ethical theory such as utilitarianism or perfectionism, and indeed Moore offered a utilitarian theory. Rawls does not, however, employ the term intuitionism in the traditional way, but rather it is 'the doctrine that there is an irreducible family of first principles which have to be weighed against one another by asking ourselves which balance, in our considered judgement, is the most just' (Rawls 1972: 34). Although Rawls breaks from normal use of the term, there is a connection between his understanding and the more traditional one: to intuit is to have an immediate awareness of the rightness or wrongness, or goodness or badness, of an action. We cannot supply reasons why an action is right or wrong, good or bad. It may be that one reason we have to weigh first principles is that those principles are simply given to us – we just know they are valid – but equally valid principles can conflict with one another. Against intuitionism, Rawls argues that we should be capable of explaining the force of first principles: a strong feeling that an action is wrong or that a principle is invalid should not preclude a rational explanation of that feeling.

Finally, we turn to what Rawls considered the main competition to his two principles: utilitarianism. To be precise, he regards one variant to be the chief alternative: average utilitarianism. Utilitarians hold that political institutions should function to increase (or maximize) the overall level of welfare – or utility – of a society. There are many variants of utilitarianism, where the difference between each depends on how utility is understood – happiness, pleasure and preference-satisfaction are the main candidates – and how it is measured, and therefore maximized. Rawls does not discuss these variants, believing they share similar weaknesses, and adopts the definition of nineteenth-century utilitarian philosopher Henry Sidgwick: 'society is rightly ordered, and therefore just, when its major institutions are arranged so as to achieve the greatest net balance of satisfaction over all the individuals belonging to it' (Rawls 1972: 22). Classical utilitarianism simply sums all instances of satisfaction regardless of the number of utility-generating beings (we have to say 'beings' because we cannot automatically exclude non-human animals). Average utilitarianism divides the overall level of utility by the number of utility-generating beings, normally understood to be human beings.

Rawls advances various objections to utilitarianism. First, while there are empirical arguments for spreading the satisfaction of utility among many people, there is no a priori argument in favour of distributive justice: if total utility is 100 units, and that is distributed among five people, then a distribution of 96 units for one person and one for each of the others is identical, in ethical terms, to a distribution of twenty units for each person. Second, if utilitarianism is distribution-insensitive, why should we be concerned with *average* utility? Average utility implies there is something ethically significant about the individual human being, such that each individual should 'count for one and nobody for more than one', to employ a formula attributed to Jeremy Bentham by John Stuart Mill (Mill 1991: 199), and yet society is treated as if it were a single person with a single life over which utility should be maximized. As Rawls argues: 'utilitarianism does not take seriously the distinction between persons' (Rawls 1972: 27). I shall return to these objections at several points in this chapter as we compare utilitarianism and the democratic conception.

As suggested earlier, Rawls's favoured democratic conception of justice is presented in two versions – general and special. The general conception is: 'all social primary goods … are to be distributed equally unless an unequal distribution of any or all of these goods is to the advantage of the least favoured' (Rawls 1972: 303). The special conception consists of the two principles of justice. Rawls hopes he can persuade the reader that the general conception would be endorsed even if the special conception, as one version of it, is rejected. The general conception is not in competition with the special conception, but, rather, the latter is a more determinate version of the former. By presenting the two principles Rawls is inviting the reader to consider the coherence and the consequences of a particular formulation of the general conception – if the two principles are not coherent or would be unstable we would have to go back to the drawing board.

Although I suggested the substance of Rawls's theory of justice changed relatively little from its initial formulation in *A Theory of Justice* to his final statement of it just prior to his death in 2002, and that it was the methodological basis of the theory which underwent the most significant revision, it would be wrong to say there were no changes of any significance in the substance of the theory. It is useful to compare the early and late formulations of the two principles:

Early formulation (1971)

First: each person is to have an equal right to the most extensive basic liberty compatible with a similar liberty for others.

Second: social and economic inequalities are to be arranged so that they are both (a) reasonably expected to be to everyone's advantage, and (b) attached to positions and offices open to all (Rawls 1972: 60).

Late formulation (2001)

First: each person has the same indefeasible claim to a fully adequate scheme of equal basic liberties, which scheme is compatible with the same scheme of liberties for all.

Second: social and economic inequalities are to satisfy two conditions: (a) they are to be attached to offices and positions open to all under conditions of fair equality of opportunity; and (b), they are to be to the greatest benefit of the least-advantaged members of society (the difference principle) (Rawls 2001: 42–3).

Although Rawls talks of two principles there seem to be three principles presented above: equal liberty, the difference principle and fair equality of opportunity. One of the changes between the early and late versions is the re-ordering of the latter two. Rawls suggests the change is merely stylistic, but I will argue that it has substantive implications (see 'Fair Equality of Opportunity', page 63). The one change Rawls concedes is significant – although he claims it is a clarification – is the presentation of the liberty principle: the phrase 'fully adequate scheme of basic liberties' is importantly different to 'most extensive basic liberty' (this is considered in 'Equal Liberty', page 56).

There is another principle of justice, missing from both of the above versions: the just savings principle (Rawls 1972: 284–93; Rawls 2001: 159–61). This principle distributes benefits and burdens of co-operation between generations, but it is important to distinguish contemporaneous and non-contemporaneous generations. The first can easily be addressed by the two principles of justice: since agents in the original position are choosing principles which are to determine their prospects over an entire lifetime, conflicts between the different age groups do not raise special philosophical problems, although more detailed social policies will have to address demographic changes such as the ageing structure of Western societies, where there is a worsening ratio of working age to retired people. Justice between non-contemporaneous generations does, however, raise a major philosophical challenge: if we say it is better to exist rather than not to exist, then we have a duty to bring a particular person into existence, but doing so may severely reduce per capita resources to the extent that we cannot assure *that person* the minimum level of resources necessary to live a decent life. And we cannot employ a veil of ignorance that denies individuals knowledge of whether or not they will exist, for the one thing of which agents in the original position cannot be denied knowledge of is the fact of their existence. Rawls argues that our duty to future generations consists in reproducing the minimal conditions for a well-ordered society and we are not required to maximize the position of the worst-off class *of all time*, only the contemporary worst-off class. This move reduces the pressure on existing generations, but it does not solve the philosophical problem, for the future population of the earth may be so great as to undermine even the minimal conditions for a well-ordered society. As we will see in pages 68–71, Rawls shifted his position on intergenerational justice, and although his later solution was an improvement on his initial one, neither is adequate.

There is a 'lexical' relationship between the principles of justice, meaning the first principle must be fully satisfied before the second principle can be applied, and within the second principle equality of opportunity must be respected before the difference principle can become operative. Rawls uses the analogy of a dictionary to illustrate lexical (or lexigraphical) ordering: all words beginning with the letter 'a' are listed prior to those beginning 'b', and within the 'a' category the words are ordered by their second letters, third letters and so on (Rawls 1972: 42). Lexical ordering is intended to avoid problems with the two main philosophical rival theories: intuitionism and utilitarianism. Intuitionists have to make judgements regarding the trade-off between values, such as freedom and equality without determinate ordering principles to fall back upon. Utilitarians settle disputes by appeal to a single principle – that utility be maximized – at the expense of the plurality of values. Lexicality entails the recognition of the plurality of values but gives some precision to their ordering. The danger, however, is that the value which is given the highest priority – in this case, liberty – will, unless defined in a relatively narrow way, trump other values. Rawls acknowledges the need for a 'limited application' of higher ranked principles if lower ranked principles are ever going to come into play (Rawls 1972: 43).

Equal liberty

Rawls, quite sensibly, does not spend long engaged in conceptual analysis – that is, trying to explain what freedom (or liberty) means independently of the value attached to freedom or to specific freedoms. He follows political theorist Gerald McCallum, who argues freedom is a triadic relationship: 'freedom is ... always *of* something (an agent or agents), *from* something, *to* do, not do, become, or not become something' (McCallum in Rawls 1972: 202*n*). While this triad may not apply to all instances of freedom, it is likely to hold for legal or political freedom, where the state is the source of unfreedom. Of course, the state also protects one individual from another and in that sense it can increase, as well as diminish, a person's freedom. For this reason, while it is generally preferable to have a greater rather than a lesser liberty – and agents in the original position are, therefore, motivated to maximize their individual shares of liberty – it is the system of liberty as a whole, rather than specific liberties, that is to be maximized. To enjoy secure liberty may require sacrificing specific liberties (Rawls 1972: 203).

   H. L. A. Hart, in an influential essay on Rawls (Hart in Daniels 1989), argued the equal liberty principle would be difficult to implement in an actual legal system because there are no criteria for arbitrating between particular liberties.* Rawls acknowledged that the singular term 'basic liberty' obscures the fact that it is a *list*, hence the revised term 'scheme' (Rawls 2001: 44). In fact, Rawls's list is similar to that found in the United Nations Declaration on Human Rights (without the articles on social rights) and the European Convention on Human Rights, and the focus should, therefore, be on rights (liberties) rather than liberty (or freedom) itself. A right protects the agent in the enjoyment of something, and while the state cannot distribute choice itself, it can distribute the *protection* of choice. Furthermore, the liberties include freedom of thought and conscience, rights to political participation, freedom of association, bodily integrity and the right to a fair trial. Some of these, especially the last one, have little to do directly with liberty in the sense of 'choice' or the satisfaction of 'wants'.

This clarification is important but we still need a philosophical derivation of the liberties, and of the lexical priority of liberty. Rawls cannot base his justification of the first principle on the fact that these liberties are widely respected in liberal-democratic societies, or that most states have signed up to conventions containing them, for agents in the original position are denied such knowledge, and denied it for a good reason: they need freely to construct the principles of justice and not rely on pre-existing moral principles or legal conventions. Rawls argues that agents in the original position will attach importance to the scheme of liberties as the means to an 'adequate development and full exercise of the two moral powers of free and equal persons' (Rawls 2001: 45). The two powers are attributed

---

* This argument requires some grasp of how the principles inform actual law-making – this process Rawls terms the four-stage. It is discussed in chapter 7.

to agents in the original position and are intended to model the rational and moral powers of real people. The powers are (a) the capacity for a sense of justice, and (b) the capacity for a sense of the good. The former means a person can understand, apply and act from, and not merely in accordance with, the principles of justice. The latter entails the 'capacity to have, to revise, and rationally to pursue a conception of the good' (Rawls 1972: 19). Equal political liberties and freedom of thought enable citizens to make moral judgements, while the liberty of conscience and freedom of association are important to forming and maintaining a conception of the good – that is, a life-plan.

The derivation of the equal liberty principle from the importance of forming a life-plan is not uncontroversial: many cultures do not attach value to personal autonomy, and would see the political promotion of autonomy as sectarian. For this reason, Rawls revised the argument for the principle in his later work, maintaining the two moral powers are 'merely political', rather than metaphysical: that is, we agree to treat one another as autonomous agents, without any further commitment to a belief in, say, freedom of the will (Rawls 1996: 420). I pursue this shift in greater detail in Chapter 8, but highlight it here in order to contrast three different derivations of the principle, which rely on three different ways of understanding the value of freedom (I owe these derivations to Carter 1995). The liberties can be regarded as *instrumentally valuable* to whatever ends individuals have. This is an empirical claim and is vulnerable to the objection that they are not in fact *equally* instrumentally valuable. In contrast, liberty could be something we value in itself, independently of whatever other ends we have – that is, liberty is *intrinsically valuable*. This seems, however, like a fetishization of freedom: committing ourselves to particular ends, such as a career or marriage, may well reduce our freedom, understood as choice, but we would surely still value our career or marriage. The third possibility is to see freedom not as intrinsically valuable, but as part of a valuable end, that is, freedom is *constitutively valuable*. A marriage freely entered into is more valuable than one forced upon a person, and so free choice is a part of the end we pursue – the end being a married state. This third position is the most credible interpretation of the value attached to freedom in the original position, but it remains sectarian – many defenders of arranged marriages would maintain they are more stable than 'free' ones, and thus provide an environment more conducive to the raising of children.

There is a presumption among liberal political theorists, and shared by Rawls, that liberty is valuable, and it is restrictions on liberty that require justification. Consequently, much discussion focuses on liberty-limiting principles. J. S. Mill famously advanced his harm principle (also known as the liberty principle): 'the only purpose for which power can be rightfully exercised over any member of a civilized community, against his will, is to prevent harm to others' (Mill 1991: 14). Other political theorists have suggested that harm-to-others (more accurately, non-consensual harm-to-others) should not be the only justification for limiting freedom – offensiveness and harm-to-self are also grounds for limiting it. Rawls says little directly on offensiveness, but he does discuss legal paternalism – state intervention to prevent an individual harming himself. Although Mill excluded children from the scope of the principle, arguing that they lacked the maturity required to make decisions, it would require a very high level of confidence in the human capacity for rational decision-making to maintain, as Mill does, that *adults* should *never* be prevented from harming themselves. On the other hand, if we take autonomy to be a foundational concept, we need some way of justifying even the occasional use of paternalism towards adults. Rawls achieves a reconciliation of autonomy and limited paternalism through the process of decision-making in the original position: although we would not select principles which implied individuals had moral duties to themselves, we would choose principles which on occasion prevented individuals harming themselves (Rawls 1972: 248–9). In effect, we consent to paternalism under some strictly circumscribed conditions. The argument can be applied to people at all stages of life, for when we choose principles in the original position we are choosing for an entire lifetime. Rational agents would, of course, restrict strong paternalism to the treatment of children, but the underlying idea of seeing your life as a whole, lived over time, informs all forms of paternalism.

Fair equality of opportunity

The second principle of justice has two parts – fair equality of opportunity and the difference principle – and as noted above Rawls changed the presentation of their order, although not their lexical relationship: equality of opportunity is lexically prior to the difference principle. Rawls's original formulation – where the difference principle was stated first, but fair equality of opportunity took lexical priority – confused many readers, and he gives no reason for setting it out in that way, or why he changed the presentation, beyond stylistic reasons. At the risk of imputing motives to Rawls, it may be that fair equality of opportunity was not seen by Rawls as a goal, but rather a constraint or proviso: the material position of the worst-off should be maximized subject to fair equality of opportunity being guaranteed. This precludes what is empirically unlikely, but still possible: that the position of the worst-off could be improved by departing from equality of opportunity. It is conceivable, albeit implausible, that lower spending on education combined with lower personal and corporate taxes would increase the income of the worst-off even as it reduced their opportunities.

Politically, equal opportunity seems uncontroversial. However, when you try to pin down the concept and establish what it requires in terms of redistribution, it becomes clear there is a continuum from a weak idea of equal access to favourable positions through to a strong notion of state intervention in family life. For example, in Britain, as in other advanced industrial countries, there is much popular debate about the social composition of the student bodies in the highest-rated universities. Students educated at fee-paying schools, or at state schools with relatively wealthy catchment areas, make up a disproportionately large part of the student intake of these universities. Even on the political right this situation is condemned: the brightest students rather than the wealthiest students should get the most desirable university places. Although politicians disagree about the causes and the solutions to this situation, there is agreement that equal access alone does not ensure a fair outcome. The difficulty is that an eighteen-year-old student has eighteen years of education and socialization behind her – every day she has been presented with opportunities of which a peer may have been denied. Those opportunities could include the emotional support necessary to achieve self-confidence and a sense of self-worth, stimulating conversation which enable her to develop a range of linguistic skills, interesting foreign holidays and activities, the presence of books in the family home, the imposition of a degree of parental discipline sufficient to encourage self-discipline, family networks and contacts, a good diet and the provision of an adequate workspace. This list could go on, and none of these items relates to formal educational provision. Even parents who do not send their children to fee-paying schools may pay for such things as ballet classes or piano lessons. In short, every day of her life for the previous eighteen years she has been given opportunities. To equalize such opportunities would require a very high degree of intervention in family life. This description of a privileged child may, of course, overstate the requirement for an equalization of opportunity. Perhaps it is not necessary that children have strictly equal opportunities, but rather each child has a *sufficient degree* of opportunity to acquire advantageous positions: this fits more closely with the idea of equality of opportunity as a constraint rather than as a goal. However, the point is that equality of opportunity is indeterminate – it does not tell us how much should be redistributed.

To make sense of Rawls's equal opportunity principle we need to distinguish formal and fair equality of opportunity. Formal equality of opportunity requires that advantageous positions – for example, college places and good jobs – are open to all and, where appropriate, allocated on the basis of talent. Fair equality of opportunity requires individuals have a *reasonable chance* of acquiring those positions. To explain the distinction between these two forms of equal opportunity, and the role that fair equality of opportunity plays within the two principles, Rawls outlines four interpretations of the second principle of justice (we assume advocates of each interpretation have endorsed the equal liberty principle). The four are natural liberty, liberal equality, natural aristocracy and democratic equality.

Natural liberty maintains careers should be open to all and wealth should be distributed through the operation of a free market, with no attempt to mitigate the effects of social class. This seems intuitively unfair, as nobody can be held responsible for his or her inherited social position. More importantly, agents in the original position are likely to select a stronger principle of equal opportunity, such that the main choice is between natural liberty and liberal equality. To illustrate the distinction between natural liberty and liberal equality consider the advantages enjoyed by university graduates in Britain. Studies have shown that in Britain male graduates earn 28% more than male non-graduates over a lifetime and for females the figure is 53% (de Vries 2014: 5). Precise percentages vary, but studies from other European countries, and North America, reveal a similar picture. Do graduates *deserve* this advantage? For advocates of natural liberty, so long as there was no institutional discrimination in the allocation of university places, any inequalities that result are justified. Defenders of liberal equality would, however, be concerned with the effects of class and family advantage. Two students may have the same entry qualifications, but if one has a relatively disadvantaged family background, while the other is relatively advantaged, the former is thought more deserving than the latter. This difference in attitude rests on a distinction between naturally derived and socially derived advantages: a natural ability, such as intelligence, is a legitimate basis for distribution, and any inequality which results from the exercise of intelligence is justified, whereas benefiting from socially inherited advantages, such as an expensive schooling, is regarded as illegitimate. In addition, what a person does with his or her natural abilities is thought morally relevant: people deserve to keep what they have acquired through their own efforts.

Rawls, however, rejects desert as the basis of distribution, and so must reject liberal equality. In part, his objection rests on the fact that no economic system allocates wealth on the basis of desert – patterns of income are determined by laws of supply and demand (Rawls 1972: 311). But he has a more radical objection:

> It seems to be one of the fixed points of our considered judgements that no one deserves his place in the distribution of native endowments, any more than one deserves one's initial starting point in society. The assertion that a man deserves the superior character that enables him to make the effort to cultivate his abilities is equally problematic; for his character depends in large part upon fortunate family and social circumstances for which he can claim no credit (Rawls 1972: 104).

This argument can only be fully assessed when we consider the relationship between equality of opportunity and the difference principle. However, two points can be made here. Rawls argues that fair equality of opportunity takes lexical priority over the difference principle, meaning we cannot distribute resources to the worst-off if that entails violating fair equality of opportunity.

But there is a problem with this argument. Rawls appears to endorse liberal equality at the stage of presenting fair equality of opportunity, while using the difference principle to go further than liberal equality, but the difference principle in fact conflicts with liberal equality: if fair equality of opportunity, interpreted as liberal equality, is lexically prior to the difference principle, then Rawls's anti-desert argument will not have any force.

This brings us back to the 'purely stylistic' revision Rawls made to the formulation of the second principle. I suggested that the placing of fair equality of opportunity ahead of the difference principle in the original formulation of the two principles implied that it functioned as a constraint on the maximization of the income of the worst-off. It may also have another, more conservative, effect, which is to invalidate reverse discrimination: the position of the worst-off may be improved if fair equality of opportunity is denied to the more advantaged, but the denial of opportunity is considered unfair. Such unfairness cannot rest on an appeal to desert – the advantaged do not, for Rawls, deserve their favoured status – but rather must derive from some idea of legitimate expectation: if you work hard you expect to be rewarded because there are public criteria for matching individual behaviour, such as performance in examinations, with the allocation of positions, such as jobs or college places.

Rawls has a choice. He could: (a) assert equality of opportunity is lexically prior to the difference principle and it rests on desert, or (b) accept equality of opportunity rests on desert, but for that reason should be overridden by the difference principle, or (c) argue for a non-desert based conception of equal opportunity. A non-desert based version of equal opportunity would, minimally, require equal access, but it is difficult to see what it would offer distinct from the difference principle. There are efficiency arguments for equal opportunity – the best qualified are likely to be the most productive – but that argument is part of the justification of the difference principle.

Finally, before turning to the difference principle, something should be said about 'natural aristocracy'. Rawls takes this idea from conservative thinker George Santayana, who argued that an aristocratic regime can only be justified if its benefits radiate out to the least well-off (Rawls 1972: 74*n*). The term aristocracy is used in a generic sense to mean rule by the best, or, more generally, that advantages should accrue to the most talented. Santayana's point, as interpreted by Rawls, is anti-individualist: the aristocracy do not, as individuals, deserve their position, but a good society is, nonetheless, structured around a hierarchy of positions. Rawls acknowledges that natural aristocracy, and with it the idea of *noblesse oblige*, is one way of interpreting the two principles of justice: an 'ideal feudal system' might try to enact them (Rawls 1972: 74*n*), and so we could endorse the two principles of justice by a method quite different to the one used by Rawls. However, the moral construction procedure (original position) assumes a post-Enlightenment conception of the human agent as fundamentally free, and as equal to other agents, whereas natural aristocracy implies natural hierarchy, and the duties which the higher social classes owe to the lower ones are derived from an organic conception of society rather than generated through the claims of individual human beings.

In summary, natural aristocracy is an interesting but eccentric interpretation of equal opportunity, and the first interpretation – natural liberty – would be rejected by most people in Western liberal-democratic societies, even in less egalitarian ones, such as the USA. Of course, the question is whether *agents in the original position* would reject these two interpretations. It seems they would, for natural aristocracy is incompatible with respect for the autonomy that characterizes the original position, and agents denied knowledge of their identities would be concerned about the inegalitarian implications of natural liberty. The real battle is between liberal equality and democratic equality. Most people in the real world endorse the former, and so the challenge for Rawls is to show that were they to reason as rational agents under fair conditions – that is, behind the veil of ignorance – they would choose the most egalitarian interpretation of equal opportunity. The credibility of this argument is best assessed after we have completed our survey of the two principles.

The difference principle

Of the three parts of the 'two' principles, the difference principle is the most strikingly original. This is in part because of its concrete political implications: it seems to provide a response to the argument that inequality is economically productive because it raises the income and expectations of the poorest in society. Politicians of the non-Marxist, social democratic left saw in Rawls's argument a principled response to the trickle-down arguments of the New Right: capitalist relations of production could be justified but they had to work to the advantage of the worst-off. To illustrate the reasoning behind the difference principle consider this income distribution table:

	A	B1	B2	C1	C2	D
Wealthy	3	70	50	120	97	250
	3	25	28	30	29	10
	3	20	23	25	24	7
Poor	3	15	15	7	10	4
Average:	3	32.5	29	45.5	40	67.75

A: Equality

B1: Maximin

B2: Maximin with chain connection

C1: Average *expected* utility

C2: Average expected utility with floor (e.g., one quarter of the average income)

D: Maximax (also: total utility – classical utilitarianism)

The table is obviously a simplification. It is intended as a way of comparing B – the difference principle – with alternative principles (the distinctions between B1 and B2 and between C1 and C2 will be explained later). Society is divided into four classes and the units represent expected annual income over an entire lifetime, with the average income indicated in the bottom row.

Rawls argues that rational agents in the original position, recognizing the seriousness of the choice, will ensure that should they end up in the bottom quartile of society they will be as well off as possible. The reasoning behind this is termed maximin: *maximum minimorum*, or the *maxi*mization of the *min*imum position (Rawls 1972: 154). Although Rawls avoids committing himself to any particular view on agents' attitude to risk only highly risk-averse agents would select B over the most credible alternative principle C2.★ To be fair, this table fails to capture the dynamic nature of income distribution, for what is presented is a one-off time slice of income, whereas in the original position agents are not choosing a *particular* distribution but a *principle* of distribution, and the principles underlying B and C2 are quite different: C2 says 'maximize average expected utility (subject to a floor)' whereas B says 'maximize the position of the worst-off'. There is a shifting sands quality to C2: it does not

★ Rawls claims to eschew any view on risk, arguing that agents in the original position face *uncertainty* rather than *risk* (Rawls 2001: 106). This seems at first sight a meaningless distinction, for uncertainty is at the heart of gambling. But developing the distinction Rawls maintains that gamblers have some knowledge of probabilities, knowledge denied to agents in the original position. This would, however, amount to denying agents *general* knowledge of society. While Rawls seeks to avoid attributing a special psychology to agents – that is, a controversial set of motivations – his argument does seem to amount to the claim that as trustees (or representatives) agents would not risk the fundamental interests of those they represent. Agents are indeed risk-averse.

concern itself with any particular group in society, but takes only average income to be morally significant. It is possible that over time distributions could move quite dramatically and compared to B the worst-off class under C2 could become a lot worse off. B, on the other hand, always gives priority to the worst-off. Nonetheless, the floor – which is defined as a fraction of the average, but could be a fraction of the income of the best-off – provides some reassurance to agents that their economic position will not be dire even if they end up among the worst-off.

Let us look at the other two distributions, and the reasoning that might lead to them. Maximax – maximize the maximum – is the reasoning behind distribution D. This is highly risky. One thing you might have noticed is that per capita income is higher in D than C, and thus one might think the average utilitarian would opt for D over C. However, we talk of *expected utility*: a maximizer wants to get the highest income possible – everybody, not just a risk-taker, wants to earn 250 units. Each person knows he has under distribution D only a one in four chance of earning that amount of money. He has a one in four chance he will end up with 4 units of income. Does his *desire* for 250 units outweigh his *aversion* to earning only 4 units? Given certain facts about human psychology – for example, that the utility from an extra amount of income diminishes the more income you have – he will reason that greater weight should be attached to the avoidance of lower incomes than the enjoyment of higher incomes. We come now to distribution A. It is *relativities* that concern someone who opts for A. Rawls argues we are not envious, and therefore we are not concerned with what other people earn, so relativities are unimportant. It might, however, be argued that if one of the primary social goods is self-respect any inequality will undermine it: there is no easy answer to this, and it does seem that for real people – as distinct from people in the original position – self-worth is (to some extent) attached to income or social status.

Finally, we need to consider the distinction between distributions B1 and B2. Two concepts are relevant here: close-knitness and chain-connection. The distribution table does not capture the first concept, which is empirical in character: if we maximize the position of the worst-off the likely consequence is that the prospects of the next poorest class will be improved. Chain-connection, on the other hand, pertains to the principle that the prospects of each class should be improved so long as the position of the worst-off is maximized and each preceding class is as well off as possible, consistent with maximizing the income of the worst-off. This argument is intended to address the criticism that a small gain for, say, unskilled workers is achieved at a significant cost to semi-skilled workers. Since agents in the original position have knowledge of economic theory, including empirical studies of economic behaviour, they will choose the difference principle in the knowledge that income redistributions are close-knit and chain-connection is, therefore, possible.

Just savings

While the benefits and burdens of co-operation can be distributed between people at a particular time there is also a temporal dimension to distribution: we consume resources *now*, but it may be at the expense of future generations. As I suggested earlier the term 'intergenerational justice' (or 'justice between generations') is used for two very different situations: justice between contemporary generations, that is, different age groups within a society, and justice between non-overlapping generations. Justice between contemporaneous generations can be addressed without great difficulty by the two principles of justice – rational agents will view their lives as a whole, and choose principles that protect them as children and when they are elderly, and they will ensure income is equitably distributed over a whole lifecycle. Justice between non-contemporaneous generations does, however, raise philosophical problems.

What makes intergenerational justice between non-contemporaneous generations such a radical challenge to Rawls's theory is that what we do today will affect not only the life prospects of future people, but whether they will exist at all. There is a consensus that population growth is a threat to the quality of life of future generations, and we have a duty to see to it that such growth is checked. But to whom is that duty owed? Imagine we have a fixed level of resources, and in World One there are five billion people, while in World Two there are twenty billion people. Average (per capita) resources will be higher in World One and its inhabitants are, therefore, better off than the inhabitants of World Two. If these are the only two worlds, is it the case that World One is the best of all possible worlds? It is not immediately obvious that it is, for one consequence of living in World One is that a large number of people would not be brought into existence. It is possible that none of World One's people would have existed if a consequence of population control is that people defer having children. Of course, uncontrolled population growth could result in some, or all, of the inhabitants of World One not being brought into existence if in World Two all children are born to, say, women under the age of twenty, whereas in World One all children are born to women over the age of twenty, but our concern is with World Two.

Agents in Rawls's original position are denied knowledge of their identities, but as Derek Parfit argues, the one thing of which they cannot be denied knowledge is the fact of their existence (Parfit 1984: 392). This creates motivational difficulties: we can be impartial between existing people but not between existing and possible people. Rawls attempts to deal with this problem by supplementing the two principles with the just savings principle. This requires each generation set aside resources for future ones. It will involve positive measures such as investing in technology, as well as negative policies such as not depleting finite natural resources. Importantly, the required level of savings is restricted to that necessary to sustain a well-ordered society (Rawls 2001: 159). There is no requirement to operate a difference principle across the generations – each generation is not obliged to identify the worst-off class *of all time*, nor is it necessary to ensure continued economic growth.

Although in his later work Rawls retains the just savings principle, he revised its derivation. He retains the idea that the principles in the original position are chosen in the present (Rawls 2001: 160).* But there is a shift in the motivational connection between generations. In *A Theory of Justice* he stipulated the generation choosing the principles of justice care for at least two subsequent generations. Rawls now acknowledges this is inconsistent with the motivational assumption of mutual disinterest (Rawls 2001: 160n). In *Justice as Fairness: a Restatement* he argues that although we assume present-time-of-entry to the original position, because we are abstracting from historical time all generations are represented. The agreement is, therefore, between all generations, and 'we say the parties are to agree to a just savings principle subject to the condition that they must want all previous generations to have followed it' (Rawls 2001: 160). Since no generation knows its place among the generations this implies all later generations, including the present one, are to follow it.

There is, however, a tension in Rawls's derivation of this principle, which Parfit quite rightly picks up on, but does not state correctly. Rather than saying persons must exist in the original position, there is a duality: in entering the original position

---

* This is the present-time-of-entry condition: agents always choose principles that will apply immediately and not be instituted at a future date or retrospectively at a past date. However, the 'present' is not a historical time, such as the time at which I am writing this sentence.

I confirm my *moral* existence, but because I do not know my generation then I cannot be sure I *actually* exist. Since the actions of one generation determine the size of a future population one of the questions which I as an agent in the original position must confront is whether I should exist. If the level of resources in the 20-billion population of World Two falls below a certain 'social minimum' then conceivably we, as agents behind a veil of ignorance, could will that *some of us* should not exist. But it is arbitrary who does exist. Detaching moral agency from actual agency has important implications for the interpretation of contractarianism. Contractarianism, even of the hypothetical variety standardly attributed to Rawls, requires a one-on-one correspondence between agents in the original position and real people – agents in the original position are their 'representatives'. In trying to deal with the problem of future generations Rawls has to break this correspondence.

Further reading

An overview of the two principles is provided by Barry (1973), Chapters 5–11 and Kukathas and Pettit (1990), Chapters 3–4. For more in-depth coverage see Daniels (1989), part 3, essays by Hart and Daniels on the equal liberty principle, and Gutmann in Freeman (2003). On the priority of liberty see Barry and Shue in Richardson and Weithman (1999; vol. 2). For a discussion of maximin, see Richardson and Weithman (1999; vol. 1): essays by Gauthier, Musgrave, Harsanyi and Cohen. Also, see Kukathas (2003; vol. 1), part 7 (utilitarianism), part 9 (perfectionism), part 10 (intuitionism); Kukathas (2003; vol. 2), part 2 (liberty and its priority) and part 9 (intergenerational justice).

5

The difference principle in focus

In this chapter I consider in greater depth the selection of the difference principle. In particular I discuss a number of objections to it, coming from what might loosely be called the political 'right' and the political 'left'. From the right Rawls is criticized for placing too much weight on the redistribution of wealth at the expense of respecting individual freedom, while from the left he is attacked for accepting capitalist relations of production and assuming that human beings are by nature capable only of limited altruism. Robert Nozick's critique of Rawls in his book *Anarchy, State, and Utopia* (1974) is taken as representative of the first position, while Gerald Cohen represents the latter position. The third writer discussed – Ronald Dworkin – advances an egalitarian theory of justice, but argues that distribution must reflect the choices individuals make – inequalities resulting from individuals' choices are justified. Finally, I round off the discussion with consideration of some empirical modelling of behaviour in the original position, and consider what that research tells us about the credibility and coherence of Rawls's theory. Although the focus in this chapter is on the difference principle, that principle must be judged as a part of Rawls's entire package of principles.

Nozick and autonomy

Robert Nozick, who was a colleague of Rawls in the Philosophy Department at Harvard University, published *Anarchy, State, and Utopia* in 1974, three years after *A Theory of Justice*. Although the book ranges widely it is often presented as a libertarian alternative to Rawls's theory. The very first line of the book sets the tone for the rest of it: 'individuals have rights, and there are things no person or group may do to them (without violating their rights)' (Nozick 1974: ix). Jonathan Wolff argues that Nozick is a one-value political philosopher (Wolff 1991: 3–4). Other philosophers accept that there is more than one value; for example, they might maintain freedom is important, but so is equality, and since freedom and equality often conflict we need a method for resolving that conflict. Rawls's *two* principles of justice express this idea. Wolff maintains that Nozick's 'one value' is private property, or, more precisely, the *right* to private property. A standard criticism of Nozick is that he asserts that individuals have rights but cannot explain their origin. He appeals to the intuition that because an individual has only one life to live that life is extremely valuable and private property rights, including the most fundamental property right, namely, self-ownership, are essential to the protection of that life. But this intuition can lead us in different directions: we might argue that nobody should be allowed to fall below a certain standard of resources. Nonetheless, even if we are unconvinced by Nozick's starting point there is much force in his criticisms of Rawls. If you do not accept the idea of natural rights, then an alternative starting point is to ask the question: if personal autonomy is very important then what are the implications for autonomy of coercively redistributing resources?

Nozick's entitlement theory of justice has three parts: (a) just acquisition; (b) just transfer; and, if required, (c) rectification. Just acquisition is concerned with how something that was unowned came to be owned, while just transfer explains the rules for exchanging that which is legitimately owned, and rectification is necessary in case either (a) or (b) is violated. Nozick follows Locke in arguing that in a world in which things are unowned individuals claim a stake to what is unowned by mixing their labour with it (Nozick 1974: 174–8). Much can be said about Nozick's use of Locke, but it is the second part of the theory which is of greater relevance for us. Just transfer is dependent upon just acquisition, for you cannot justly transfer what you have not justly acquired, and acquisition is a very strong idea – it entails full control over the thing which is acquired, including the power to transfer it to another person. Nozick takes the example of the great basketball player Wilt Chamberlain (Nozick 1974: 161). Chamberlain was at the time of Nozick's writing greatly in demand by basketball teams. He signs an annual contract in which it is agreed that twenty-five cents from the price of each ticket goes directly to him. People 'cheerfully' attend games at which Chamberlain is playing, dropping a separate twenty-five cents in a box with Chamberlain's name on it. We suppose that in a season one million people watch Chamberlain play, and so Chamberlain ends up with $250,000, a much larger sum than the average income. Is Chamberlain entitled to that money? Nozick argues that so long as Chamberlain did not use threats or fraud to acquire each amount of money (twenty-five cents) then his additional earning is legitimately his by a simple transfer (Nozick 1974: 161–3). The fact that such transfers will over time create significant inequalities is irrelevant, for what matters is that individuals have consented to the transfer. Those who object to such transfers want 'to forbid capitalist acts between consenting adults' (Nozick 1974: 163).

To evaluate the force of Nozick's argument we need to compare his theory of justice with Rawls's theory. Nozick divides theories of justice into two groups – end-state and historical (Nozick 1974: 153–5) – with a sub-division of the second into patterned and unpatterned theories (Nozick 1974: 155–60). End-state theories are not concerned with what people *do*, but only with the *end-result*. Utilitarian theories fall into this category – the aim is to maximize total, or alternatively, average utility. Historical theories, on the other hand, connect distributions with what people have done. For example, distribution according to desert is a historical principle. Such theories can be further divided into patterned and unpatterned theories. Any principle which involves the phrase 'to each according to ____', where the blank is filled in as 'desert', 'need', 'labour' and so on, is going to generate a pattern (Nozick 1974: 159–60). Nozick characterizes Rawls's theory as patterned: priority to the worst-off (maximin) generates a pattern. Nozick calls his own theory unpatterned, because whatever distribution exists should be the result of choice. You could argue that this is patterned with the blank filled in as (rights-protected) 'choice', but choice is not really the same as desert or need or maximin – the latter two provide objective criteria that can be used by a redistributive agency (the state) whereas you choose to do whatever you like. Certainly, the state can distribute the protection of choice by enforcing private property rights, and there is a pattern to the distribution of such rights, but the exercise of those rights will generate patterns which should, for Nozick, be beyond the control of the state.

Individuals may, under Nozick's utopian framework, aim to bring about an end-state or patterned distribution, but what may not happen is that the state *coerces* people into creating that end-state or pattern. To appropriate some of Chamberlain's $250,000 is tantamount to forcing him to labour (Nozick 1974: 172). Rawls makes two important points against Nozick. First, against the charge that taxation is forced labour Rawls argues that a distinction must be drawn between the arbitrary seizure of property and the legitimate expectation that certain incomes attract certain levels of taxation (Rawls 2001: 52). Although political institutions – the legislature and executive – can change the rules, they must if they are to be deemed just change in accordance with publicly recognized standards (here the formal constraints of right are very important – see page 41). Chamberlain is free to alter his behaviour according to the taxation laws. Second, in Nozick's example a great deal of weight is placed on the fact that the spectators consented to the transfer, and his defence of such a transfer implies that interference through taxation is not simply a violation of Chamberlain's rights, but also a violation of the spectators' rights. Rawls argues that each of a series of transfers could be just without the outcome of all transfers taken together being just. In part, this is because there are third parties affected by the transfer who have not consented to the inequalities generated by the transfers. Rawls draws a distinction between two kinds of rules, those that regulate the basic structure over time and are designed to preserve background justice from one generation to the next and those that apply directly to the 'separate and free' transactions between individuals and associations. The conjunction of these two types of rules generates an 'ideal social process' view, in contrast to Locke's (and Nozick's) 'ideal historical process' view (Rawls 2001: 54). Rules regulating the basic structure are chosen in the original position and interpreted by institutions. Within those rules individuals are free to enter contracts. Taxation is a necessary part of the maintenance of a just society.

Whatever the adequacy of Rawls's response Nozick's critique does throw light on the tension between the difference principle and the other principles of justice, including the principle of fair equality of opportunity. On the one hand, Rawls stresses human autonomy, and this is expressed as the ability to institute and revise a life-plan. Fair equality of opportunity is important as a means of giving value to the package of liberties which constitute the first principle. The difference principle is, however, disconnected from the actions of individuals: individuals will receive benefits regardless of what they do. I would adapt Nozick's objection to Rawls by arguing that patterned theories of justice are not in themselves incompatible with the exercise of personal autonomy but, when a society seeks to bring about a particular pattern of justice *independently of individual choices*, there is a tension between autonomy and distribution. Even if we endorse a relatively extensive state – distinct from Nozick's minimal state – we must still ensure freedom and equality cohere. Rawls believes the two principles, lexically ordered, do cohere: freedom – or a scheme of liberties – takes priority over equality, but equality is necessary for the liberties to be of equal worth. Understood in this way, the difference principle is of instrumental, rather than intrinsic, value: equality (or the limitation of inequality) is not a good in itself, but the outcome of providing individuals with the material goods necessary to exercise effectively their scheme of liberties. In short, we should not care about patterns. But if the liberties are what matter, then it is plausible to argue that a guaranteed social minimum (without chain-connection) is sufficient to ensure effective exercise of the equal liberty principle, and the difference principle is either redundant or may, in fact, undermine personal autonomy. The extent to which it does so will depend on the more precise social policies that are enacted, but the thought is that passive recipience of social welfare benefits corrodes self-reliance and initiative. I return to this issue in pages 86–91, but first I want to consider an attack on Rawls from a rather different political perspective.

Cohen and motivational instability

Marxists have tended not to engage in debate with liberal thinkers such as Rawls, rejecting as they do certain liberal claims about the nature of human motivation and political epistemology. On human motivation, Rawls maintains the principles of justice apply to a society characterized by moderate scarcity in which people are in conflict over the distribution of those scarce resources. A Marxist would maintain that when production levels reach a certain point – and capitalism is historically useful because it massively increases productivity – we will be in a position to say that there is no longer scarcity and the causes of social conflict will be removed. Regarding political *epistemology* – that is, how we *know* what is just – Marxists maintain that it is only in a post-scarcity situation that we will be able to determine the correct distribution of resources. Gerald Cohen is unusual amongst Marxists in his engagement with liberal (and libertarian) thinkers such as Rawls and Nozick. Cohen's first book, *Karl Marx's Theory of History: a Defence* (1978), defended Marx from a highly orthodox position but within the methodological framework of analytical philosophy – that is, positivist social science, and especially rational choice theory. Since writing that book Cohen has abandoned his orthodox Marxism, but not his analytical approach. He ascribes the shift in his position to the recognition (shared by many other Marxists and ex-Marxists) that the working class is not a vehicle for social, and therefore *ethical*, change, and there cannot be material abundance such that we are taken out of the circumstances of justice (Cohen 2000: 112–15). So long as there is moderate scarcity there will be a need for theories of justice, and thus socialists must engage with liberal political theory, and not dismiss it as the ideological expression of a capitalist society.

Cohen advances three key objections to Rawls's argument. First, Rawls has an incoherent model of human psychology, or motivation. Second, he restricts the principles of justice to the basic structure of society, and that conceals exploitation. Third, Rawls rejects self-ownership as morally irrelevant to the distribution of resources (curious as it may seem, on this point Cohen sides with the 'right-wing' libertarian Nozick against Rawls).

The first two objections are closely related to one another. People in the original position are motivated to maximize their share of the primary goods but from behind a veil of ignorance, meaning that while they are self-interested, they are forced by the way the original position is set up to be impartial. Rational people will, Rawls argues, select the two principles of justice, including the difference principle, which entails maximizing the position of the worst-off (maximin). The original position is intended to model how real people *could* behave: we take account of the strains of commitment to the principles of justice. The difficulty is that the theory itself pulls in two different directions: on the one hand, Rawls assumes that we – that is, 'we' in the real world, and not in the original position – can develop a commitment to giving priority to the worst-off in society, and the difference principle is the structural device by which this is achieved. But how much the worst-off *actually receive* will depend on everyday human behaviour. Recall the distribution table on page 65, under maximin (with chain connection) the richest quartile of society get fifty units and the poorest quartile get fifteen units. Imagine you are in the top quartile. What motivations will you have in the real world, assuming you endorse Rawls's theory? First, you will be committed to giving priority to the worst-off and so will regard a system of taxation and redistribution legitimate, but, second, you will be motivated to maximize your income. These two motivations do not necessarily conflict if we assume, as Rawls does, that inequality generates incentives to produce and thus help the worst-off. But if you are really committed to helping the worst-off do you not have a moral duty to give *directly* – not just through taxation – to the poor, and also work to bring about a society in which the poorest receive more than fifteen units?

Cohen borrows a slogan from the feminist movement: the 'personal is political' (Cohen 2000: 122–3). How you behave in your personal life is a political issue. Rawls, along with most liberals, rejects this claim, arguing that the distinction between public and private is essential to a pluralistic society, and not all aspects of morality should be enforced by the state: while it is right to require people to pay taxes to help the worst-off, it is for individuals to decide what they do with their post-taxed income. This may not resolve the tension which Cohen identifies between, very crudely expressed, public generosity and private avarice, but the onus is on Cohen to explain the role of the state in promoting private generosity. Cohen talks about 'encouraging an ethos' in which people seek to bring about a more equal distribution of resources (Cohen 2000: 131), but it is unclear how this is to be achieved: is the state the agent of ethical change, or do we rely on non-state forces? If we rely on the state, then how can a *coercive entity* bring about a change in voluntary behaviour? Certainly, state policies can change behaviour – there is plenty of empirical evidence showing this to be the case – but political theory seeks to justify principles and behaviour independently of coercion. Orthodox Marxists hold that human motivations change with material conditions, and that a coercive state will be unnecessary in a post-scarcity economy, and this assumption releases them from having to rely on the state to coerce people into changing their behaviour. Nonetheless, whatever the weaknesses of Cohen's own position, his criticism of Rawls carries weight – there is a tension within the moral psychology of the agent between public egalitarianism and private acquisitiveness, and we need to explore this further by considering Cohen's second criticism, which relates to the basic structure.

For Rawls, the rich fulfil their duties to the poor by accepting the legitimacy of taxation, and those tax receipts are used to fund certain institutions, such as the pre-university education system, money transfers (social security and pensions) and healthcare. Outside the scope of the original position is a private sphere, which includes the family. Rawls accepts that the family is a major source of inequality – the transmission from parent to child of privilege undermines equality of opportunity (Rawls 1972: 74). But because liberty (the first principle of justice) takes priority over equality (the second principle) there has to be a legally protected private sphere. Not only is the private sphere a source of inequality it also produces within itself inequality. Here Cohen joins forces with feminist critics of Rawls, such as Susan Okin: families are based on a division of labour, and one loaded against women, and because the recipient of redistribution is the household (Okin 1989: 92), and not the individual, there is a class of people – mostly women – who are worse off than that class which Rawls identifies as the worst-off.

The impression left by Rawls in his earlier work was that intra-familial distributions were outside the scope of a theory of justice. He later clarified his position, arguing that while social justice regulates the basic structure and does not apply directly to, or regulate internally, the institutions which make up the basic structure, the principles of justice do affect the nature of those institutions, so 'to establish equality between men and women in sharing the work of society, in preserving its culture and in reproducing itself over time, special provisions are needed in family law (and no doubt elsewhere) so that the burden of bearing, raising, and educating children does not fall more heavily on women, thereby undermining their fair equality of opportunity' (Rawls 2001: 11). Rawls is, however, very unclear about the implications of taking gender equality seriously, and this lack of clarity derives in part from the vagueness of the boundaries of the basic structure.

Cohen argues that what Rawls includes in the basic structure is arbitrary – Rawls cannot give clear criteria for what should or should not be included. Rawls cannot say that the basic structure consists of those institutions which are coercively enforced – that is, institutions we are forced to fund through taxation – because the basic structure is defined *before* we choose the principles of justice, whereas what is coercively enforced is a decision to be made in the original position (Cohen 2000: 136–7). Cohen has identified a major difficulty with the basic structure argument: it determines how the original position is set up, but it has the effect of excluding from the discussion in the original position important ethical considerations. Although the agent in the original position is a representative of an individual human being, the recipient of income is a household – so the fifteen units the worst-off receive accrue to the agent's household and not to the agent. In addressing this criticism we need to separate substantive and methodological questions. Understood as a substantive problem about the details of Rawls's principles of justice, a resolution might be at hand: instead of income going to households it should go to (adult) individuals in the form of a 'citizen's income', which all adults receive regardless of whether they are employed or not. There are several problems with such a proposal. First, it implies the state has a role in determining intrafamilial distributions of income and so corrodes the private sphere. Second, it may act as a disincentive to work and raises what Rawls terms the Malibu problem – that is, people get benefits regardless of whether or not they work, thus undermining the idea of society as a co-operative venture (Rawls 2001: 179; see page 92). The Malibu problem could be avoided by establishing that citizens only get a guaranteed income if they are carrying out domestic labour, such as child-rearing, but then again the state would have to intrude into family life in order to ensure that this was the case. Third, the effect of a citizen's income might be to reduce economic activity and so worsen the position of the least favoured class in society. These are substantive problems, but Cohen's criticisms are aimed at a deeper, methodological level.

Cohen argues that the basic structure implies a division within the moral psychology of the agent between public and private morality and, crucially, that division is unstable. There are several possible responses to this charge. We could say 'so what?' – life is full of motivational tensions, and a tension does not necessarily render a set of principles incoherent, or even unstable. The alternative is to accept there is a problem with Rawls's model of human motivation, but we resolve it by replacing the difference principle with a guaranteed social minimum, and change the motivational assumptions behind redistribution: we no longer say that the income differential between rich and poor is only justified if it is to the advantage of the poor, but rather once a guaranteed social minimum has been achieved we abstain from making any moral judgements regarding the pattern of distribution. As I argued earlier (page 77), we should not be concerned with patterns because equality (or the reduction of inequality) has no independent value. In short, we do the opposite of what Cohen argues we should do, and we weaken the egalitarianism of Rawls's theory.

To complete the discussion of Cohen's critique we need to consider his final major objection: Rawls does not take seriously the idea of self-ownership. Marx argued that the workers do not get the full value of their labour. This argument assumes there is something a person owns that generates a moral right to other things: in effect, as a Marxist, Cohen, along with Nozick (who is not, of course, a Marxist) endorses Locke's mixed labour formula. What Cohen rejects is the idea that mixing your labour establishes merely first acquisition. For Locke and Nozick, once the world is privatized the mixed labour formula ceases to be of any use. Cohen argues that a worker *constantly* mixes his or her labour, such that there is a continuous claim on the product. He rejects Locke's claim that 'the turfs my servant has cut are *my* turfs' (Locke 1992: 289). Insofar as the servant (wage-labourer) does not get the full value of his labour he is exploited, and the resulting distribution is unjust. Rawls implicitly rejects the notion of self-ownership. That does not mean we do not have rights over our bodies, but rather we have no *pre-social* rights; the rights we have are the result of a choice made in the original position. This becomes clearer if we look at the concept of desert, which I briefly discussed in pages 59–65.

Desert is tied to effort: we get something if we do something. Rawls argues that we are not responsible for our natural endowment – strength, looks, intelligence and even good character – and so we cannot claim the product generated by that natural endowment (Rawls 1972: 104). Under the difference principle one person may earn fifty units and another fifteen units, but not one unit of that thirty-five unit difference is *justified* by reference to desert. Of course, in *causal terms*, the difference may be attributed, at least in part, to native ability, but that does not justify the difference. Rawls goes so far as to say that natural endowments are a social resource to be used for the benefit of the worst-off (Rawls 1972: 179). It is strange that on desert Rawls is the radical, whereas Cohen sides with Nozick. It is true that Nozick does not believe that the rich are rich because they deserve to be rich – Wilt Chamberlain is rich because *other people choose to give him money* to play basketball – but the idea of self-ownership (private property rights) does imply a right to keep the fruit of your labour. Cohen is not the first writer to observe the tension in Rawls's theory between personal autonomy, and therefore responsibility for choice, and his rejection of desert-based distribution. But Cohen's argument has a slightly different focus: if we reject, as Cohen and many feminists do, the sharp distinction between public and private then we need some alternative basis for distribution, and one which guarantees respect for the individual.

Despite distancing himself from orthodox Marxism, Cohen implicitly appeals to Marx's labour theory of value; a theory which itself drew upon, but criticised, classical liberal–capitalist thinkers such as David Ricardo, Adam Smith and John Locke. Cohen believes that people have the right to keep certain things, and this is based on the labour-time which they have expended in producing those things: insofar as the worker does not receive the value of his labour he is exploited. But the labour theory of value is implausible. Thomas Nagel argues that the value of a product is not the result of the amount of labour which went into it, but rather, it is the other way round: the value of labour is the result of the contribution that labour makes to the product (Nagel 1991: 99). Ask yourself this: if you have a firm making smartphones which group of workers do you *least* want to lose? The canteen staff? Cleaners? Assembly line workers? The smartphone designers? Venture capitalists? It could be argued that the last two groups are the most important. The conclusion to be drawn is that if we want to justify an egalitarian distribution of wealth we need what Rawls attempts to offer, which is a moral justification which assumes that many of the poorest will get *more* than that to which their labour 'entitles' them.

Applying the insights of both Nozick and Cohen we can identify a number of related tensions in Rawls's theory of justice. Rawls argues that individuals are motivated to accept as just those principles which they would have chosen under conditions of fairness, that is, in the original position, and the capacity to institute and revise a life-plan is crucial to the fairness of the original position. So we have a very strong conception of human autonomy at the heart of the theory. Yet the difference principle is unconnected to the capacity for choice – it is a pattern to which agents must conform, rather than being a pattern generated by the choices agents make. Furthermore, although I (hypothetically, in the original position) choose the difference principle, the moral motivation to accept redistribution is in tension with the desire to maximize my income. Such motivational stress will be inevitable so long as we distinguish public and private morality, but it is exacerbated by the fact that, i*n terms of public morality*, income differences are not connected to individual choice, whereas, of course, the choices individuals actually make do determine what people get. These problems are connected to a third aspect of Rawls's derivation of the principles of justice: the nature of the goods that are subject to distribution.

Dworkin and resourcism

Since human beings possess more than one attribute or good, it is possible that equality in the possession of one will lead to, or imply, inequality in another. For example, Anne may be able-bodied and John disabled. Each could be given equal amounts of resources, such as healthcare, and so in this regard they are treated equally, but John's needs are greater, so the equality of healthcare has unequal *effects*. If Anne and John were given resources commensurate with their needs, they would be being treated equally in one sphere (needs) but unequally in another (resources). So when we talk about equality we need to know what it is that should be subject to distribution. The two main positions in the 'equality of what?' debate are equality of welfare (welfarism) and equality of resources (resourcism).

The term 'welfare' is used in the economic sense (welfare economics) rather than in the more everyday sense of welfare provision – it is possible to construct a welfare state around resourcism. If we are concerned with equality of welfare then the focus is on well-being, which is measured either by 'good' mental states, such as happiness or pleasure, or by the extent to which an individual's preferences are satisfied. Resourcism, on the other hand, does not focus on subjective states but rather on goods, such as Rawls's primary goods. The standard criticism of resourcism is that it fails to take into account individuals' differing abilities to convert equal resources into comparable levels of well-being. This may arise because a person is born with disabilities, or more controversially because he has expensive tastes. This criticism could be dismissed as simply the reassertion of welfarism: it assumes that equality of *welfare* is what matters. But if we say that welfare is not what matters then resourcism looks fetishistic – we have these resources, but they are unconnected to the desires of real, living human beings. In response, a resourcist could argue that people should be held responsible for at least some of their preferences and the insensitivity of resource allocation to well-being reflects the importance of personal responsibility. The difficulty for Rawls is that while his theory is strongly resourcist the difference principle gives no moral weight to personal responsibility.

Ronald Dworkin takes up the idea of resourcism but seeks to address this problem of ambition insensitivity in Rawls's theory (Dworkin 2000: 30). Dworkin wants the allocation of resources to reflect certain things: (a) you should not be disadvantaged by those things that are beyond your control, and that includes your innate abilities, social class (insofar as you did not determine it) and everyday bad luck (together he calls these things 'circumstances'); and (b) it is legitimate for resources to reflect the choices you make, such that we distinguish choices and circumstances (Dworkin 2000: 28–9). He argues that distribution should be circumstance-insensitive but choice- (or ambition-) sensitive. To develop an alternative theory of distribution Dworkin works with two linked ideas: the hypothetical auction and the hypothetical insurance system.

Starting with the hypothetical auction we imagine a group of shipwrecked people ('immigrants') washed up on a desert island with abundant resources and no native population. The immigrants have equal personal resources (circumstances), but differing tastes. They endorse the principle that no one is antecedently entitled to any of the resources, and instead they shall be divided equally between them. They also accept what Dworkin calls the 'envy test': 'no division of resources is an equal division if, once the division is complete, any immigrant would prefer someone else's bundle of resources to his own bundle' (Dworkin 2000: 67). A problem, however, emerges which evades the envy test: the bundles might not be equally valuable to each person given differing tastes. In other words, each person gets an identical bundle of goods, but because individual tastes differ they may not attach equal value to them – they do not envy other people's bundles, but nonetheless they would rather have a different bundle.

To deal with this problem the immigrants set up an auction. Each immigrant is given an equal set of clamshells, to be used as currency. We assume the goods have been created, but it is open to any immigrant to propose new goods. The auction proceeds, with prices set and bids made, until all markets have been cleared – all goods are sold – and the envy test passed. Of course, individuals might be lucky or unlucky in their tastes. If there is high demand for goods which are in short supply then the price of those goods will be high. Dworkin argues that taking responsibility for our lives means accepting our tastes, or if necessary adjusting them, and not expecting that resources will be redistributed to satisfy those tastes (Dworkin 2000: 69–70). It should be added that the products we bid for can include leisure – if one person chooses to work twelve hours a day, and another opts for a leisurely four hours, then the income difference is the price paid by the latter person for eight hours of leisure. If he were to look simply at the income of the hard worker then he might feel envy, but the envy test requires a whole life comparison: the hard worker has lost something by being a workaholic.

A crucial assumption of the auction is that the participants enter on equal terms – they differ only in their tastes. Resources are equal, meaning we all start with the same number of clam-shells, but our personal resources are also equal: nobody is, for example, severely disabled. It does not take much reflection to see that people are not born equal in personal resources, and on the desert island itself it would not be long before there was an inequality of resources, and the possibility that the envy test will not be satisfied. Luck will play a part, but Dworkin makes a distinction between calculated gambles and brute bad luck. You might, for example, take all reasonable precautions but still contract lung cancer. Alternatively, you may be a heavy smoker and as a result contract cancer: the smoker took a calculated gamble and lost (Dworkin 2000: 74–5).

Since the immigrants on the desert island know luck will play a significant role in their lives and they are rational in the sense of being prudential – adopting a whole life perspective – they will insure themselves against misfortune, such that among the products for which they bid will be insurance policies. Of course, individuals are free to buy different policies, but because we assume that risk is random – let us say the chances of a coconut falling on your head from a great height is pretty much equal for all individuals – the premiums will be the same for each person, and so the insurance market will reflect the choices people make. The problem comes when we introduce identifiable brute luck – that is, we know from the day someone is born, and in fact even before he is born, that he will have a poor natural endowment.

To deal with this problem we agree to randomize risk. Although Dworkin does not use the term, in effect he argues for a veil of ignorance, albeit one much 'thinner' than Rawls's: an individual knows his talents but does not know the price those talents command in the market (Dworkin 2000: 94). Dworkin wants the agent to know enough about his or her talents and preferences to make judgements about the appropriate level of insurance cover to buy. The difficulty is that even when we are denied knowledge of the price our talents can command, the insurance premiums can never match the income a talented person will acquire through the exploitation of his or her talents. Not everyone can earn as much as J. K. Rowling earns (in 2008 £170 million) and although buying an insurance policy which will pay out £170 million may at first sight seem the rational approach, further reflection shows it to be irrational. Let us assume that Rowling is in the 99th income percentile, but at the time she selects an insurance policy she does not know she will earn £170 million per year – imagine she is returned to the state of being a struggling writer trying to get her first book published. We also assume that once the veil is lifted the actual pay-out will equate to what the market can bear and that she will be obliged to pay whatever premium she has agreed. If the market can bear coverage to the 30th percentile and Rowling has taken out a policy which covers her to the 90th percentile, and she remains a struggling writer on let us say the 35th percentile, then she will be far worse off than if she had opted for a cheaper policy. Importantly, the wealthy Rowling (on the 99th percentile) is also worse off, as she has to keep writing these Harry Potter books just to cover her premiums (Dworkin 2000: 98). The aim of Dworkin's argument is to calculate how much income should be transferred across classes and he does not suggest that poor people have to pay the premiums, but in order to work out how much wealth should be transferred agents behind his 'veil' must assume they will be obliged to pay up.

No insurance system will fully compensate a person for lacking talent, or, more accurately, lacking *marketable* talents. What an insurance system does achieve is a means of justifying contingencies: as Rawls argues, life is a lottery, but agreeing to principles of justice – or agreeing to the *unequal distribution* of resources – entails accepting that certain contingencies can legitimately affect a person's fortunes. For Rawls the only way such contingencies can be justified is if they work to the benefit of the worst-off. The importance of Dworkin's hypothetical insurance model lies in what it reveals about the logic of that position – we can never fully compensate people for their poor endowment, such that the difference principle must operate as a partial compensation. A society in which redistribution of wealth is perceived as only partially compensating for inequalities in natural endowments is necessarily unstable – the poor are likely to be resentful of *any* inequality, but the attempt to eliminate, as it were *finally*, all inequalities will destroy the conditions for the development and exercise of talent.

Rawls frequently uses the concept of reciprocity, although he is not consistent: sometimes it means mutual advantage (Rawls 1972: 178), and at others a refusal to take advantage of one another (Rawls 1972: 14). Furthermore, he talks of human beings' natural talents as a 'common asset' the benefits of which we share (Rawls 1972: 101). Combining the ideas of reciprocity and common assets, and applying Dworkin's insurance model, there is a more positive way of justifying inequality as the price *we agree to pay from a standpoint of moral equality* for the mutual enjoyment of natural talents. Such an idea also accords much more closely to everyday intuitions about the fair distribution of resources than the reasoning which Rawls claims would lead agents in the original position to endorse the difference principle. In the last section I consider some evidence to support this claim.

Experimental approaches to justice

Norman Frohlich and Joe Oppenheimer offered the first experimental analysis of Rawls's theory of justice. Using students in Texas, Maryland, Manitoba and Poland, they sought to test the proposition that rational agents would choose the two principles, and specifically, the difference principle. They offered the research subjects four principles of distribution: maximize average income with a *floor constraint* (guaranteed minimum); *maximum income* (average utilitarianism); maximize income with a *range constraint* (ratio of the lowest to the highest income); *maximin* (Rawls's difference principle). The subjects were first presented with these four principles, which they were required to rank. Possible income distributions – similar to those presented on page 65 – were included in the explanation of the principles. After subjects had presented their rankings, they explored the implications of the principles experimentally through random assignment to one of the four income classes. Once this had been done for each of the principles the subjects were then asked (once again) to rank the principles.

This first stage was conducted by individuals alone, but the second stage involved a collective, or group, choice of principles. The group was given an incentive – in the form of higher pay-offs – to reach unanimous agreement. Of the eighty-one experimental groups only one group chose the difference principle (maximin). The breakdown of choices was:

Floor constraint	78%
Maximum income	12%
Range constraint	9%
Maximin	1%

The experimental set-up can be criticized and in fact subsequent experiments have provided stronger support for Rawls's principle (Mitchell et al 1993: 631). Frohlich and Oppenheimer did not, for example, distinguish merit and efficiency arguments for inequality. They do test the stability – in Rawls's sense – of principles of justice by asking subjects to correct a piece of text, with payments 'taxed' according to the different principles (Frohlich & Oppenheimer: 47–8). This reveals the effects of taxation on productivity, but does not distinguish merit and efficiency: do we reject a principle of distribution because it lowers productivity or because it is unfair that those who work hard do not keep more of their income? If the intention of a theory of justice is to separate different normative concerns, then an experiment which fails to do so can be deemed invalid.

However, while the experiment did not formally separate merit and efficiency arguments the informal comments of the subjects suggests merit plays a role in the reasoning behind the overwhelming selection of the floor constraint principle, even if the comments are sometimes ambiguous, with references to 'incentives' or 'encouragement' (Frohlich & Oppenheimer: 83). The consensus among political theorists is that desert can play no role in the distribution of resources. Sometimes this rejection of desert borders on contempt for everyday morality. But if there is strong support for merit or desert – and especially if endorsed through a reflective experiment – then it is important to consider the reasons underlying this position. I would suggest two, both of which rely on the importance of reciprocity and talent sharing outlined at the end of the last section. First, there is the Malibu problem: can people refuse to work and then claim their share of primary goods under the difference principle? As Rawls puts it: 'are the least advantaged ... those who live on welfare and surf all day off Malibu?' (Rawls 2001: 179). Rawls's answer to his own question is to include leisure time as a primary good. If we include sixteen hours per day as leisure time and therefore eight hours as work time, then so long as meaningful work is available to the surfers they are receiving an extra eight hours of leisure. Consequently, they cannot be counted among the worst-off: 'surfers must somehow support themselves'. At base, Rawls's theory assumes that citizens are 'fully co-operating members of society over a complete life' (Rawls 2001: 179), such that to refuse to work when able to do so undermines the stability of the political system.

The second social consequence of autonomy relates back to Dworkin's insurance model. I suggested that his argument does not achieve what he aims at, which is to distribute according to choice rather than chance: it is impossible to have taxation levels (equivalent to 'insurance premiums') which enable everybody to receive the income of a J. K. Rowling. But there is another way to use the insurance model: the difference between the rich and the poor – that is, the gap which cannot realistically be bridged through the insurance premium – has, at least, two components. The first is, as Dworkin suggests, explained by the choices people make, but the second is the price we are willing to pay for living in a society where there are people capable of developing their talents. This argument on its own would amount to nothing more than a defence of market-based resource allocation, but combined with a selection of insurance premiums behind a veil of ignorance it can be turned into a different kind of argument: we do justice to individuals by validating inequality from behind a veil of ignorance.

Further reading

Kukathas and Pettit (1990), Chapter 5 addresses the libertarian critique of Rawls. The following essays discuss the difference principle in some detail from various perspectives: in Richardson and Weithman (1999; vol. 2), see Sen, Van Parijs and Cohen; in Freeman (2003) read Daniels and Van Parijs. See also Kukathas (2003; vol. 2), part 3 (difference principle) and part 5 (equality), and Kukathas (2003; vol. 3), part 1 (libertarian perspectives), and part 2 (Marxist perspectives).

6

The original position in focus

Why enter the original position? Or, to re-phrase the question: why be moral? In attempting to answer this question we are not trying to convince people of the advantages of moral behaviour, but rather attempting to demonstrate that it is not irrational to act morally. However, even if we can provide an adequate account of morality we still have to explain how morality and coercion can be reconciled, and this raises the problem of political obligation: how can morally autonomous agents submit to a coercive authority? In several places in *A Theory of Justice* Rawls appeals to the logic of the prisoner's dilemma to explain why we are morally bound to the state – why, for example, we ought to obey unjust laws (Rawls 1971: 350). Yet as I suggested in Chapter 2, the logic of the resolution to the prisoner's dilemma is only a starting point for Rawls, for there are multiple alternative resolutions. Moral conflict, and not simply the possibility of self-interested free-riding, threatens the stability of the political system.

Central to the credibility of Rawls's responses to these two questions is his conception of the human agent as autonomous. As suggested in pages 35–39, he distinguishes rational and full autonomy, where rationality is defined as the ability to institute and revise a life-plan – or pursue a conception of the good – and full autonomy is the capacity to pursue that good within moral constraints. Real people, Rawls implies, do not separate rational from full autonomy, but to provide a coherent theory it is essential they are separated in the original position. If the agent is, so to speak, 'split apart' in the original position the challenge then becomes one of putting the agent back together in the real world: if we cannot live by the principles we have (hypothetically) chosen, then the credibility of the whole theory must be called into question. As in the last chapter, I approach this problem through discussion of a number of critical perspectives.

Sandel and communitarianism

Michael Sandel in an influential critique of Rawls's theory – *Liberalism and the Limits of Justice* (1982★) – argues that the Rawlsian conception of the agent (or self) is incoherent. Sandel begins with a distinction between the self and its ends. Because we are denied knowledge of our identities in the original position the self must, in some sense, be prior to its ends (where 'ends' include values, relationships and activities). This primacy of the self over its ends is connected with three other kinds of primacy, so we have four in total:

1. The primacy of the self over its ends (Sandel 1998: 54).
2. The primacy of volition over cognition (Sandel 1998: 59).
3. The primacy of the right over the good (Sandel 1998: 17).
4. The primacy of justice over other virtues (Sandel 1998: 15–16).

★ A second edition of the book appeared in 1998. While the 1982 text is reproduced the 1998 edition contains an important new Preface clarifying the alleged communitarianism of the argument and a response at the end to Rawls's later 'political liberalism'.

If the self is prior to its ends, morality has a volitional rather a cognitive character: we *choose* rather than *discover* principles of justice. And if morality is volitional then rightness, or procedural correctness, rather than goodness (that is, the pursuit of virtue) characterizes the individual's relationship to his own life. The corresponding *social* relationship is one of justice as the first virtue of social institutions: the key characteristic of justice is that it pertains to relations between agents who are in conflict with one another over the distribution of material resources and have opposing conceptions of the good. In a society where justice has primacy, the state is legitimate insofar as its laws and policies are couched in terms that are neutral between those conflicting conceptions of the good, rather than justified by appeal to any particular conception of the good.

If Rawls is committed to all four relations of primacy then we end up with a weak, indeed incredible, conception of human agency: just as neutrality between people means the state must not favour a particular conception of the good, so the agent must be neutral between different conceptions *within his own life*, with the consequence that he is incapable of making any choices (Sandel 1998: 161–4). Sandel, in fact, arrives at this 'incredible' conception of the human agent by running together two mutually exclusive understandings of liberalism. The first, which can be termed liberalism as neutrality, avoids making any claims about how the agent relates to himself – it does not matter how people decide how to live their lives so long as they respect each other's rights. The state is legitimate if it acts as a 'neutral umpire' between competing and conflicting interests. The other understanding, which can be termed autonomy-based liberalism, maintains the legitimacy of the state depends on protecting and promoting a particular model of human agency, so that not all ways of life are equally valuable. Although autonomy-based liberalism does not necessarily force people to be free, its policies will promote some ends at the expense of others, and so, by extension, it assumes *rational* agents will judge some ends to be inferior to others. It follows that Rawls's understanding of the agent is not, as Sandel suggests, absurd, but nonetheless Rawls must make clear whether his is a neutralist or an autonomy-based liberalism.

Sandel's own position has been labelled communitarian because it implies human beings must be motivated to pursue some goods, chief among which is civic friendship (Sandel 1998: 180–1). This is highly underdeveloped and open to criticism but the inadequacy of Sandel's own model of agency does not release Rawls from the charge of incoherence, and indeed a consideration of it can be informative for our discussion. At the heart of Sandel's argument is the *axiological* relationship of the self to its ends – that is, how do we come to attach *value* to a relationship, set of beliefs or way of life? While in the first edition of *Liberalism and the Limits of Justice* Sandel implied that community, or civic friendship, was the source of value, in the second edition he rejects this interpretation of his argument. The communitarianism that he believes has been wrongly attributed to him holds that determining what is just 'always takes the form of recalling a community to itself, of appealing to ideals implicit but unrealized in a common project or tradition' (Sandel 1998: xi). Such a view of ethical justification leaves the ends of action uncriticized. The ends are simply the values that happen to obtain in our society – communitarianism is cultural relativism. Rather than assert the priority of the right over the good, as Sandel claims liberals do, or the priority of a contingent good over the right, as communitarians do, what is required is 'that principles depend for their justification on the moral worth or intrinsic good of the ends they serve' (Sandel 1998: xi).

We can summarize Sandel's critique of Rawls: selfishness is not the main motivational problem in Rawls's theory, but rather it is the failure to provide an adequate account of how people come to value things, such as a way of life or personal relationships. Because agents are denied access to their particular values in the original position but have strong attachments outside it the only way Rawls can conceive of social unity is as neutrality between conflicting values (or conceptions of the good). That neutrality is, however, too weak to motivate people to respect the principles of justice. The neutrality of the political system is built on an instrumental theory of individual rationality: Rawls defines rationality as the most effective means to given ends, such that the ends are beyond rational assessment (Rawls 1972: 143). He does allow that some ways of life are inferior insofar as they manifest a lower level of complexity – this he terms the Aristotelian Principle (Rawls 1972: 426). But Sandel argues this is inadequate, for it amounts to a merely *formal* principle of rationality, whereas, human beings need access to *substantive* values, capable of motivating them to act. These values reflect constitutive attachments between people – they define what a person is, rather than being, as the original position implies, external to the person's identity. Sandel argues that:

> To imagine a person incapable of constitutive attachments … is not to conceive an ideally free and rational agent, but to imagine a person wholly without character, without moral depth. For to have character is to know that I move in a history I neither summon nor command, which carries consequences none the less for my choices and conduct. It draws me closer to some and more distant from others, it makes some aims more appropriate, others less so. As a self-interpreting being, I am able to reflect on my history and in this sense to distance myself from it, but the distance is always precarious and provisional, the point of reflection never finally secured outside the history itself. A person with character thus know that he is implicated in various ways even as he reflects, and feels the moral weight of what he knows (Sandel 1998: 179).

What is interesting about this passage is its ambiguity: on the one hand, there is an acknowledgement on Sandel's part that to be a rational agent you need to distance yourself from the values which you have acquired through socialization, hence terms like 'self-interpreting being', 'distance' and 'point of reflection'. But to avoid conceiving of the self as existing prior to its ends, he stresses the importance of 'constitutive attachments', 'character', 'moral depth' and 'history'. While Sandel's alternative model of human agency and motivation is weak, his critique is important in identifying a major tension, or antinomy, in the Rawlsian model, summed up, albeit unintentionally, in the ambiguous language of this quotation. By antinomy is meant a contradiction between two necessary requirements of rationality: the requirement that there should be substantive values to pursue, and the requirement that we challenge or question those values. To explore further this antinomy I want now to consider a different critical perspective on the Rawlsian method for deriving political principles: the feminist critique.

Gilligan and feminism

Although there are different strands of feminist thought, a concern of many feminists is the need to recognize the diversity of moral experience. The *care* a mother shows for her children represents a qualitatively different kind of moral interaction to the *impartiality* which citizens are required to show to one another in the allocation of rights and resources. A full moral theory must encompass these different moral experiences – and, by extension, different sources of motivation – and not give priority to one particular type of experience at the expense of others. In this section I consider the work of one important writer whose work challenges the priority given to impartiality in Rawls's work.

In her book *In a Different Voice* (1982) Carol Gilligan makes no mention of Rawls, and it may seem odd to call it a critique of his theory. However, the book – which is an exploration of experimental moral psychology – was very influential in what became termed the 'ethics of care' debate, where an ethic of care contrasts with a Rawlsian ethic of impartiality. Gilligan presents a critique of psychologist Laurence Kohlberg, whom Rawls quotes approvingly, although without claiming that a philosophical theory, such as his theory of justice, is dependent on empirical moral psychology (Rawls 1972: 460–1*n*). Kohlberg argued that moral development in children went through six stages: essentially, the child begins from a situation of egoism and moves to the recognition of the reality of others, initially through self-interest ('I'll be *punished* if I don't behave myself') through to the internalization of norms ('I *ought* to act in a certain way'). Morality is an achievement: you step out of your own shoes and put yourself in the shoes of another – morality is about impartiality, fairness, justice. It is not difficult to see that the original position models a Kohlbergian moral psychology.

Gilligan, who as a research assistant at Harvard University was carrying out experiments with children and young adults for Kohlberg, found that females responded to his thought-experiments in a qualitatively different way to males: they spoke in a different voice. Faced with the choice between stealing drugs from the pharmacist or seeing your wife die, two eleven-year-olds (Jake and Amy) asked by the researcher to put themselves in the shoes of the person (Heinz) making this choice responded in different ways. For Jake it is a conflict of rights – the pharmacist versus Heinz (or his wife) – whereas for Amy, it is about complex relationships. And while Jake seizes on the story with enthusiasm, Amy implicitly demands more context (Gilligan 1982: 26–7). If morality is fundamentally concerned with how we relate ourselves – our *selves* – to others, then the female voice begins with connection to other, that is, with relationships, and sees morality as a breaking of that connection. And there has to be a break because conflict cannot be avoided. The male voice begins with the isolated self, and morality – or fairness – is the way a connection with other selves is established (Gilligan 1982: 26). The self-descriptions, after prompting by the researcher, of Jake and Amy further illustrate the distinction in voices. Jake talks about the place he lives, his father's occupation, his views of the world and how tall he is; he locates himself in time and space, but separates himself by listing his abilities, beliefs and height. Amy talks about her likes and dislikes, but locates herself in terms of relationships (Gilligan 1982: 35). Gilligan cites the research of sociologist Janet Lever to show how males relate to one another through the abstract medium of rules: Lever observed children's games and noted that boys' games were more complex, involved more players and lasted longer. Girls' games were simpler and shorter. When disputes arose the tendency was for the boys to refer to rules, settle the dispute and start the game up again, whereas for girls the dispute ended the game (Gilligan 1982: 9–10).

Gilligan draws a number of philosophical conclusions from these experimental data. The ethics of impartiality, which under-lie Kohlberg's experimental set-up, excludes identification with the emotions of others, including feelings of empathy, sympathy and compassion. Rawls's original position models a particular type of moral experience, namely, the capacity through role-reversal to recognize the force of other people's interests, but without any emotional identification with others. The exclusive focus on role-reversal is dubbed an ethics of impartiality, while the recognition of emotional identification is termed an ethic of care. These labels may, however, mislead: Gilligan is not reject-ing impartiality as a form of moral motivation, but, rather, is claiming that exclusive focus on impartiality marginalizes 'care', and crucially, as argued above, women are much more likely to see human relationships in terms of care than impartiality. However, while not rejecting impartiality, she does regard the two ethics as conflicting with one another. This conflict parallels that between autonomy and constitutive attachments identified at the end of the last section, for it involves a tension between closeness and distance from other people. The key difference between the communitarian and feminist critiques is that the former still relies on a monistic conception of morality – that is, a single unified conception of moral agency and motivation – whereas Gilligan defends a pluralism not only of values, but also of forms of moral reasoning.

There are at least two ways in which Gilligan's empirical findings can be construed as a challenge to Rawls's method for deriving political principles. The findings could suggest that justice is a gendered concept, such that the thinking modelled by the original position is masculinist. Alternatively, the results of her work do not reveal a gendered response to moral questions but they do show how motivationally thin Rawls's theory is: there are *politically significant* relationships between people that cannot be captured by the concept of impartiality. In the remainder of this section I want to consider the first – 'justice is gendered' – argument.

Owen Flanagan and Kathryn Jackson argue for compatibility between impartiality and care. They note that Gilligan's findings reveal both genders (or sexes) give their highest impartiality responses to the Heinz example. This implies experimental subjects employ a division of labour between different moral problems rather than seeing problems from a distinct gendered perspective. Impartiality and care are perspectives which both genders can adopt. The important question is why a particular perspective is adopted. It may be a reflection of the background situation of the moral problem – some problems demand an impartial perspective, others favour an ethic of care. Or it could be that as individuals are socialized they come to adopt a particular perspective, and while they can grasp alternatives, their default position is one of either impartiality or care: there are cognitive costs to switching perspectives, such that men might *tend* towards impartiality, and women towards care. Such cognitive economy does not preclude the possibility of recognizing different reasons for action: *Heinz* should steal the drug because it will save *his* wife, and the wife should get the drug because any human life is more important than the pharmacist's bank balance (Flanagan and Jackson 1987: 626).

That both men and women can adopt the two perspectives goes some way to ensuring that reasoning from the original position could be androgynous, but if there are powerful social – and perhaps also genetic and biological – forces predisposing men and women to distinct default positions then a conflict arises when the veil of ignorance is lifted. I started this chapter with a discussion of the split in the moral psychology of the agent: a split between the un-self-knowing agent in the original position and the self-knowing agent in the real world. I argued that the credibility of Rawls's theory of motivation depended on explaining how the split agent is reconstructed. If men tend towards impartial reasoning then the task of reconstruction is for them much easier, and crucially their ability to advance their interests through the exercise of the two principles of justice is much greater than for women. In short, not only do women have a more difficult psychological task, but they will also end up in inferior social positions. Gilligan cites the work of Nancy Chodorow, who argued that young boys and girls have a similarly strong attachment to their mothers, but that as they get older they tend to identify with the same-sex parent, with the result that while girls intensify their caring orientation, boys have to work towards a separation and the resulting identification with the father is not a replication of the initial boy-mother relationship (Gilligan 1982: 7–9). That not all boys and girls follow these respective paths does not invalidate the claim that there are powerful forces predisposing men and women to different default orientations.

Kohlberg has struggled to deal with the challenge posed by Gilligan's work (Flanagan and Jackson 1987: 631–6), but Rawls is not under the same pressure. In part, this is because Kohlberg is presenting an empirical theory of moral development, whereas Rawls does not need to take a position on these empirical questions – an alternative theory to the one presented by Kohlberg may support Rawls's theory of motivation. More importantly, Rawls's account of motivation is restricted to the political sphere, even though it must be compatible with private motivations, meaning that it must be possible for people to live by principles of justice. Kohlberg, on the other hand, offers a comprehensive account of moral motivation, one which purports to explain not only obligations to the state and fellow citizens, but also parental obligations to children and relationships between friends. He does, however, advance one argument against Gilligan which is useful for Rawls's limited, political, account of motivation: justice must have primacy over care, for the experience of fairness and the development of the disposition to be just are necessary to the formation of care. This priority should not be understood as a causal claim, for as Rawls acknowledges, the family is the first school of moral sentiment: children experience caring before they experience justice. But, rather, it is a logical claim: the ethic of care must entail relationships between beings capable of mature reflection, such that there is an asymmetrical relationship between parents and (young) children, whereby children experience care, and to a degree respond to it, but they do not have a full understanding of caring. Nell Noddings, a leading exponent of care, acknowledges as much when she says the cared-for recognizes the carer so that a relationship of reciprocity exists (Noddings 2002: 19). Reciprocity implies justice, or impartiality, so that behind caring there exists a framework of justice. If we apply this claim to the two children debating what Heinz should do, we come to the conclusion that whereas Amy sees the problem as breaking a human relationship, and thus moving from care to impartiality, Jake sees the problem as making a connection, and so moving from impartiality to care. There is a mutual entanglement of impartiality and care, even if there is a gendered *direction* of motivation. Impartiality is, however, primary, because while it is possible to imagine a pure impartialist it is impossible to imagine a carer who lacks any conception of fairness, or role-reversal. The key point is that political philosophy follows the logical structure of concepts, and the logic of care and of impartiality suggests the former is dependent on the latter. That said, if we accept the priority of impartiality over care we might still be forced to recognize a conflict between the two and an adequate theory of justice must be capable of accommodating the two ethics. It ceases then to be an issue of gender and becomes a broader problem of human relationships. It is this broader problem we need to consider.

Nagel on the personal and the impersonal

Thomas Nagel's work has focused on the relationship between two standpoints: the personal and the impersonal. In his main work on political theory – *Equality and Partiality* (Nagel 1991) – he argues that these two standpoints are seemingly irreconcilable, although given changes in human motivation the political conflict generated by the clash between them may be lessened. Nagel is very close to Rawls intellectually and for that reason his work is useful as both sympathetic criticism and a source of arguments for resolving some of the tensions in Rawls's theory of justice. While *Equality and Partiality* is of greater direct relevance to political theory, I want to use Nagel's first book, *The Possibility of Altruism* (1970), as a framework for the discussion of the later work, and of Rawls's theory of justice.

In that early work Nagel does not regard the two standpoints as conflicting, and indeed altruism – the ability to be moved to act by other people's interests at the expense of one's own

– is made possible by the relationship which a person has to himself. Just as my life is merely 'one among many' so 'now' (this moment) is just one time among many: if I can be moved to act by recognition of my future (that is, act prudentially), then I can also be motivated to act in the interests of other people (act altruistically). Although Rawls draws on both of Nagel's ideas (Rawls 1972: 190–1, 422), he does not put them together, and this is a shame, because Nagel's argument provides a useful way of understanding the motivational demands of the original position. Using Nagel, we can say that the original position is not merely a heuristic device for discovering what justice would require of us under certain hypothetical conditions, but actually models facts about the nature of human beings, namely their capacity to adopt two interconnected perspectives on their lives: prudence and altruism. Morality is rational because it is derived from a perspective we must necessarily adopt towards our lives. Importantly, to be concerned about other people we do not have to believe in any metaphysically suspect collective entities, such as the Marxian idea of species-being. Altruism – or impartiality – is a characteristic of *individuals*.

This interpretation of the original position only works if we maintain that both altruism *and prudence* are rational requirements, and there are aspects of Rawls's theory of motivation in the original position which conflict with prudence. He does argue for temporal neutrality (prudence): 'rationality implies an impartial concern for all parts of our lives … the mere difference of location in time, of something's being earlier or later, is not in itself a rational ground for having more or less regard for it' (Rawls 1972: 293). But his basic theory of rationality is desire-based, meaning it is rational to satisfy one's desires. If we define desire as an affective (or emotional) state of wanting something, then by its nature desire is rooted in the present. Although we may talk of future desires, they are simply desires which we *might* have and cannot be granted the same status as present desires.

To illustrate the point, Nagel asks us to imagine that he – Nagel – will be in Rome six weeks from now (t +6), and that he will at that time have to speak some Italian (Nagel 1970: 63). Nagel will desire to speak Italian at t +6, but the question is whether he now has a reason to act in such a way as to satisfy that future desire, and that means having a reason regardless of whether he has a present desire to satisfy that future desire (Nagel 1970: 64). Nagel may now have a present desire to satisfy his future desire by enrolling in an Italian class, but the future qua future has no force on his reasoning as evidenced by the fact that were he to have no present desire to satisfy his future desire he would have no reason to enrol in the Italian class. Desire may always be present in motivation, because to be motivated is to desire something, but it does not follow that desires always explain reasons for action – the recognition of one's future, or of other people's interests might create a desire that did not exist prior to that recognition. It is important to differentiate these motivated desires from basic, or unmotivated, desires, which just come upon us.

Nagel acknowledges the argument is abstract – in order to act we need some substantive ends, and if desire does not supply those ends then what does? We could follow Sandel's argument and posit certain objectively valuable (cognitive) ends, such as family life, challenging work or intellectually stimulating play, but we could not show that people are *irrational* if they do not pursue these ends. Rawls has followed the dominant tendency in political theory, which is to avoid any particular theory of value; he uses the word desire, which implies an affective state, but he could substitute the word preference, which is a cover-all term embracing cognitive as well as affective ends. This would be an avoidance strategy: we assume people have ends, which may come from diverse sources, such as emotions or recognition of the objective value of certain things external to the mind, and rationality entails pursuing the most effective means to the satisfaction of those preferences. The problem is that this ties the value of the primary goods – those supposedly all-purpose means for the satisfaction of ends – to the preferences which people happen to have. Given that people have diverse sets of preferences – we do not all want the same things in life – the primary goods cannot have the same value for all agents. This indeed is the crux of the feminist critique of Rawls: men and women do not want the same things, and they do not therefore attach equal value to the primary goods. Yet the coherence of the original position depends on holding those goods to be equally valuable for all agents.

Making coherent the original position requires postulating a theory of rationality that holds some preferences to be irrational. To avoid relying on a list of objectively valuable ends, those preferences would have to be deemed irrational because they are incompatible with a perspective the agent must *necessarily* adopt on his life. An agent who acted on preferences which were seriously detrimental to his future interests would be irrational because he failed to recognize the conditions of his own agency. As Nagel suggests, if we can show that a person's future interests can motivate that person to act, it follows that the interests of other people might also motivate action. But a corollary of this argument is that the emotional states bound up with the idea of care – which we can take to be a form of altruism – must be susceptible to challenge. This does not mean that caring is irrational, but, rather, the ethic of care must be subject to rational criticism. At this point, we need to turn to Nagel's later work, in which he is much less confident about the compatibility of the two standpoints and where although he does not discuss feminist criticisms of impartiality, he does implicitly recognize their force.

Even in his first book Nagel acknowledges that a reason for action may contain what he there called a free agent variable (later termed an agent-relative value) (Nagel 1970: 48). To illustrate the role of an agent-relative variable I will take the earlier example of Heinz, but I will give his wife a name: Mary. The two children, Jake and Amy, might justify the theft in one or more of the following ways:

(a) The act will prolong Mary's life.
(b) The act will prolong her life.
(c) The act will prolong someone's life.

Reason (b) is subjective: it is a reason *for* a particular individual. Reasons (a) and (c) are, on the other hand, reasons for the *occurrence* of things, and so objective. These differing descriptions of the person who will benefit from the theft of the drug are important for how we understand the veil of ignorance, which is Rawls's device for ensuring impersonality. Although the aim of the original position is to create general principles, and not to determine individual action, the credibility of the theory depends upon people respecting principles, such as the right to property. In the Heinz example, the pharmacist's property rights might be violated. Could we select a principle which would permit a *legitimate transfer* of resources, such that Heinz obtains the drug? How would we frame such a principle? We could not reason that a named person should get the drug, for that would violate impartiality. But agents in the original position are motivated to advance their own interests, and so there must be some way of expressing the personal. When the two children, Jake and Amy, are asked what they would do, the implication is that they should engage in role-reversal: What would *I* do if *I* were Heinz? Likewise, in the original position *I* ask what *I* would want, rather than asking what *any* person would want. This distinguishes the original position as a first-person choice procedure from a utilitarian choice by an impartial judge. Critics, such as Sandel, argue there is no difference between this supposed first-person choice and the impartial judge, for the agents in the original position are identically situated. Sandel is wrong: a judge simply aggregates preferences. Even if the judge then applied a principle of equal distribution, he cannot recognize any fundamental conflicts between agents. By forcing us to adopt the first-person standpoint of each agent we are confronted with a conflict.

Whereas in *The Possibility of Altruism* Nagel thinks that subjective (or agent-relative) reasons can be subsumed under an objective principle – if I want the drug then I must necessarily want anybody to have the drug – he now argues that agent-relative and agent-neutral reasons may conflict. This affects the possibility of motivation in the original position. We need to adopt a first-person standpoint in the original position in order to explain motivation: I am motivated to respect principles *I* have chosen in the original position. But the 'I' is ambiguous. It could mean me (a particular person) or it could mean anybody. Imposing a veil of ignorance does not resolve the conflict, for while we do not know our identities we know we represent particular people. What makes Nagel's argument so powerful is that these two standpoints – the personal and the impersonal – presuppose one another (Nagel 1991: 14). While he now maintains they conflict, he has not abandoned the idea of a necessary connection between them. To illustrate, take the example of the parent–child relationship. Few people would dissent from the assertion that 'parents should show special concern for *their* children', such that Philip is not acting wrongly when he bestows love and material resources on his son James. If an observer were asked to justify Philip's actions he could employ proper names (Philip should care for James), pronouns (he should care for him), roles (parents should care for children) or, more naturally, roles plus a possessive pronoun (parents should care for *their* children). While it is impossible to justify a *principle* of parental concern by employing proper names, as in the first statement and (elliptically) in the second statement, Philip's concern for James cannot be derived reductively from the only statement that is purely objective: that 'parents should care for their children'. I believe that advocates of an ethic of care have something like this in mind when they say an ethics of impartiality illegitimately marginalizes important moral relationships. But Nagel's insightful study of moral motivation reveals the interconnectedness of objectivity and subjectivity: in caring for his son, Philip does recognize other parents are justified in showing special concern for their children, so that the fourth statement, which combines subjective and objective descriptions of the agents, is closest to the reasoning impartial agents deliberating from a *first person* standpoint should adopt. It does not, however, resolve the conflict between the standpoints, for given scarce resource parents will compete on behalf of their children.

Natural duty and political obligation

I began the chapter with two questions: is it rational to be moral? And, if we are capable of moral motivation why accept that coercion is legitimate? Rawls employs two concepts that are intended, at least implicitly, to answer these questions: natural duty and political obligation. Natural duties exist independently of any voluntary act. There are many types, some positive and others negative. Examples include the duty to help another person so long as the cost to oneself is not excessive; the duty not to injure or harm another; and, the duty not to inflict unnecessary suffering (Rawls 1972: 114). Politically, the most significant is the duty to create (and to uphold) just institutions. If there is such a duty then it must exist prior to any decisions made in the original position, and we need therefore to explain its origins. Many interpreters of Rawls simply assert that such a duty exists and appeal to the everyday sense of justice as proof of its existence. But I would argue that the persuasiveness of Rawls's theory depends on having an account of the structure and origins of this duty. If Rawls's theory is to be genuinely constructivist, then the natural duty must be formal rather than substantive – we cannot maintain the idea that procedures validate outcomes *and* insist that pre-contractual moral sentiments underlie the chosen principles. Of course, Rawls is modelling everyday attitudes towards the distribution of goods and so there are such sentiments 'out there in the real world', but the original position is intended to convey the idea that structural features of ourselves and our relations to other people motivate us to act, even if we are unaware of the existence of any such structure. In other words, we look at the world and see that people do often (but not always) act justly. We then need to establish whether attitudes and actions are *simply* the product of socialisation into a particular culture or whether there are features of human agency that explain them.

Kant, who is the biggest single influence on Rawls's theory of justice elaborated this structure in terms of human autonomy: I am required to act (only) in accordance with a maxim that I can will should be a universal law (Kant 1996: 73). I should be motivated by something that lifts me above my animal nature and through which I prove my freedom to myself. Moral sentiments must be the *product* of autonomy. Nagel's explanation of motivation in terms of the recognition of the equal reality of different times and the equal reality of different lives is a less metaphysically demanding version of the Kantian categorical imperative, and again amounts to a structure which explains moral sentiments. As Nagel acknowledged in his later work, both theories – Kant's categorical imperative and his own argument from prudence-altruism – suffer from what might be termed hyper-objectivity: if we abstract too far from desires (or sentiments), we lose contact with the personal standpoint. And a role-reversal argument, such as Nagel's or Rawls's, must hold to some idea of the personal standpoint: I must see the world through *your* eyes.

In his later work Rawls distanced himself from any metaphysical (or structural) interpretation of moral motivation, arguing that a theory of justice appeals to ideas of political, and not comprehensive, liberalism. That argument is discussed in detail in Chapter 8, but I want here to pursue the possibility of using Nagel's later argument as the basis of the natural duty to create and uphold just institutions. Nagel stresses that the personal and the impersonal interpenetrate: a father is partial towards his children, but recognizes that other fathers (and parents) can reasonably feel the same way about *their* children. The recognition of the impersonal *within* the personal does not, however, make the original position coherent, for it establishes no limits on either personal or impersonal concern. We might recognize both standpoints, but how much weight should we attach to each? Is there a rational trade-off between them? Nagel argues that in some situations there is no conflict: at a party we would not fight over the last chocolate éclair even if we are both extremely fond of chocolate éclairs. But imagine we were in a boat, and each of us had a son or daughter, and there was only one child's life-jacket left: it would be extremely difficult, and possibly wrong, to suppress the partiality we feel towards our children and give up a claim to the last life-jacket (Nagel 1991: 24–5).

A theory of justice is, of course, limited to the basic structure of society, and does not provide guidance on how to behave in either trivial or tragic circumstances. Indeed, one of the aims of the theory is to create the social conditions in which we do not have to make tragic choices – the stability of the principles depends upon favourable conditions. However, even under favourable conditions, there might be a conflict between the personal and the impersonal. The desire of many wealthy parents to do their best for their children may motivate them to buy educational advantages for those children, even though they know this could harm the prospects of other children. The existence of positional goods – goods the enjoyment of which depend on excluding others – intensifies this conflict. Weak as this may sound the best that might be achieved is a setting of parameters. Some acts of partiality are clearly acceptable, such as the bestowal of love onto children, and others are clearly not, such as nepotism in the awarding of jobs or business contracts. But in between there may be a huge area of dispute. At the very least, interpreting the choice in the original position as a role-reversal exercise modelling structural features of human beings – that is, their capacity to be motivated by other people's interests – allows us to assess the force of sentiments of justice.

Rawls places great stress throughout his work on the possibility that human beings can be *motivated* to respect the principles of justice, and he pushes to the background the fact that the principles must be coercively enforced. He does make clear that coercion will be necessary, and accepts the logic of the prisoner's dilemma. Indeed, the fact of coercion affects what it is reasonable to demand of people. Acknowledging the role of coercion does not, however, constitute a justification of it. Whatever doubts there may be about the coherence of Rawls's theory of motivation – and I have spent most of this chapter discussing these – if we accept that human agents can act morally we then need to explain why they should cede a degree of moral autonomy to the state. It is important to recognize disobedience to the state is motivated not only by calculations of self-interest, but also by moral judgements at variance to the judgements of the state. In short, Rawls needs a theory of political obligation.

In contrast to a natural duty, an obligation, Rawls argues, only exists in the context of just institutions. We have no obligation to obey laws and policies emanating from unjust institutions. In addition, obligations must be self-incurred. But as Rawls acknowledges, this renders political obligation impossible: since we are born into, rather than given the choice to live under, the state there can be no act which binds all citizens. Nonetheless, he does employ the concept of political obligation and although I think his argument is confused it is worth exploring, especially as it sheds light on the broader issue of moral motivation.

Rawls lumps together obligations associated with accepting an office under the constitution with the enjoyment of the benefits that arise from living in a well-ordered society. Both types of obligation normally apply to relatively privileged groups of people, but there is an important distinction between them: office-holding generates obligations peculiar to that office, whereas the obligations supposedly incurred by the wealthy are generated simply by enjoying the primary goods. If the wealthy accept they have a *natural duty* to uphold a redistributive system, why should they have an *obligation* on top of that natural duty? Rawls anticipates this objection, and argues for a distinction between 'those institutions or aspects thereof which must inevitably apply to us since we are born into them and they regulate the full scope of our activity, and those that apply to us because we have freely done certain things as a rational way of advancing our ends' (Rawls 1972: 343–4).

If we accept the claim that all benefit from living under a state, but we are only bound to it if the fruits of co-operation are fairly distributed, and that requires giving priority to the worst-off, then it could be argued that *all* 'freely do certain things' as a rational way of advancing their ends simply by exercising the rights and opportunities afforded by the principles of justice. In effect, we have an argument equivalent to Locke's King's Highway defence of obligation: we tacitly consent by using the state's resources. The difference from Locke would be that the background principles of justice are fair. If the background institutions are just, and coercion is required to assure one another that nobody will take unfair advantage of those institutions, then it is hard to see why each individual does not have a moral obligation to obey the state.

There are three possible reasons why Rawls maintains a distinction between natural duty and obligation, and holds that all citizens have a natural duty to create and uphold just institutions, but not all have an obligation to obey the state. The first argument rests on a distinction between negative and positive duties: natural duties are negative, whereas obligations are positive. Rawls talks of having a natural duty *to comply with* laws, but an obligation to *carry out* the duties of an office (Rawls 1972: 344). This distinction has an intuitive appeal with regard to the special obligations of office, but breaks down when applied to the more general activities associated with being a citizen: complying with laws often requires quite specific positive acts, while the obligations incurred by 'taking advantage' of co-operative arrangements may not entail identifiable acts. Rawls talks of the privileged having a sense of *noblesse oblige*, which, apart from the oddness of such a concept as part of a morally and politically egalitarian theory, generates no determinate duties (Rawls 1972: 116).

The second argument relates the natural duty/obligation distinction to the stabilization of the political order. Agents in the original position must be assured that the real people they represent will develop an effective sense of justice, and that commitment to principles of justice will deepen over time. If we can assure one another we are committed to the principles then stability will be assured. And here we appeal to the principle of fairness (or reciprocity): if we take advantage of institutions, we have an obligation over and above our natural duties to sustain those institutions. The use of the language of obligation makes explicit that commitment and thus reinforces the institutions. This is a valid argument, but it is dependent on the coherence both of the principles and the procedure through which they are constructed: if the underlying principles or procedure are incoherent then this is likely to be felt at the level of everyday belief and practice.

The weakness of the reciprocity argument becomes clearer when conflicts arise between moral autonomy and state authority, for then natural duty and obligation come apart: natural duty may require that we disobey the law, while political obligation entails obedience to law. I argued earlier in this section that Kant was the most important influence on Rawls, and he should have used a Kantian argument to explain why we have a pre-contractual natural duty to create and uphold just institutions. But it is Kant's *moral theory* that explains the natural duty and we cannot, by definition, be coerced into acting morally. In his *political theory* Kant argues that those subject to law need not be morally autonomous, for while a coercively enforced constitution is intended to create the social conditions for the exercise of moral autonomy, the state is concerned merely with the protection of external freedom and not the direct promotion of internal freedom (or autonomy). Indeed, the dictates of the state may well be contrary to the requirements of morality. Despite the possible conflict between moral autonomy and political subjectivity, Kant maintains we have an unconditional obligation to obey the state, on the grounds that there can be no *private* judgement of right, where 'right' is a condition in which each person respects the other person's negative freedom, a freedom made concrete by private property rights.

We can contrast Rawls and Kant by making a distinction between motivation-dependent stability and enforcement-dependent stability. Kant's politics is grounded in external freedom, meaning, the freedom secured from others – a security guaranteed by submission to the state. Rawls, on the other hand, grounds his theory of justice in the public recognition on the part of each citizen of a sense of justice, and the stability of the political order depends upon it. Although Rawls makes much of the 'fact of coercion' as a background condition against which we choose principles of justice, he avoids discussion of the possible conflict between moral autonomy and coercion. He implies political obligation is a developmental concept: the more people benefit from living in a just society, the greater are their obligations to obey the state. The problem is that his argument places enormous stress on the willingness of agents to comply with the principles of justice. Perhaps more importantly it depends on providing a coherent account of the moral standpoint, and I have questioned the coherence of that standpoint.

Further reading

There is a considerable body of secondary literature on the themes discussed in this chapter. Starting with the communitarian critique of Rawls, see Kukathas and Pettit (1990), Chapter 6; in Richardson and Weithman (1999; vol. 4), see Sandel, Gutmann and Alejandro; in Freeman (2003), see Mulhall & Swift. On liberal neutrality, read Raz, and Kymlicka in Richardson and Weithman (1999; vol. 5). On moral development see articles by Kohlberg, Bates and Gibbard in Richardson and Weithman (1999; vol. 4). Feminist analysis is provided by Nussbaum in Freeman (2003), and Okin in Richardson and Weithman (1999; vol. 3). See also Chapter 5 of Okin (1989). On Kantian constructivism see O'Neill in Freeman (2003); Johnson, Darwall, Galston and Brink in Richardson and Weithman (1999; vol. 2). See Kukathas (2003; vol. 1), part 8 (Rawls and Kant); Kukathas (2003; vol. 3), part 3 (feminism) and part 5 (communitarianism).

7

Civil disobedience and punishment

Most of *A Theory of Justice* is concerned with what Rawls calls ideal theory. That is, he assumes for the purposes of his argument that people comply strictly with the principles to which they have agreed. He departs from this assumption only in his discussion of civil disobedience, which can be defined, at least initially, as morally justified law-breaking. It is only in a society where there is partial, rather than strict, compliance with the principles of justice that civil disobedience has a role. Principles of justice are selected unanimously in the original position, but the principles are general in nature, and so we need a mechanism for generating more specific laws in the real world. Although a variety of law-making procedures are available it will be impossible to avoid majoritarian procedures, and majoritarian democracy always carries the danger that majorities will oppress minorities. Civil disobedience arises under conditions in which a partially just society passes unjust laws: the civilly disobedient make appeal to the sense of justice of the majority. In a (fully) just society there would be no need for civil disobedience and in an unjust society there is no sense of justice to which you can appeal.

As well as considering civil disobedience I will also discuss Rawls's justification for punishment. Civil disobedience and punishment are coupled together because they are both parts of non-ideal theory: we punish people who are not complying with the principles of justice, or, more accurately, with the laws that conform to those principles. The necessity for a theory of punishment follows from the fact that principles of justice will be coercively enforced, such that there must exist sanctions. Rawls does not discuss punishment in *A Theory of Justice*, or indeed in any subsequent work, so we have to turn to an early work, 'Two Concepts of Rules' (1955; in Rawls 1999b).

Majority rule

Rawls begins his discussion of civil disobedience with an apparently paradoxical claim: we have a duty to obey unjust laws, but we are also morally entitled, and possibly have a duty, to disobey unjust laws (Rawls 1972: 350–1). To understand this we need to consider the structure of Rawls's theory. The principles of justice are chosen from a position in which people are morally equal (the original position). But the chosen principles are general in nature – they do not take the form of constitutional rights, or concrete laws, and *laws* are the object of civil disobedience.

There are several stages between the agreement to principles of justice and the creation of laws, and what happens between these stages is crucial to our understanding of Rawls's argument for civil disobedience. Rawls sets out a four-stage sequence:

1. Original Position
2. Constitutional Convention
3. Legislative Stage
4. Judicial Stage

We are already familiar with the original position, so let us consider the second stage. Once the principles are chosen, we need to apply them to real societies. We are to imagine a constitutional convention in which members are denied knowledge of their own identities, but have knowledge of their society. Delegates at the convention are charged with producing a constitution that conforms to the two principles of justice.

Rawls's treatment of the third stage is somewhat unrealistic. He imagines the 'ideal legislator' to be a person who passes statutes that conform to the constitution, but from the standpoint of denial of knowledge of his or her identity (Rawls 1972: 198). A more realistic view would be that as we move down the sequence of stages the veil of ignorance is progressively lifted, such that at the constitutional stage the delegates know their society but not their individual identities, and at the legislative stage they know both their societies and their identities. If we accept this revision to Rawls's four-stage sequence, then at the legislative stage there is a battle for votes, organized by political parties in a majoritarian electoral system. The danger is that what has been chosen at the first two stages – the principles of justice and the constitution – are jettisoned at the legislative stage in favour of the straightforward clash of competing interests, and the possibility that the majority will oppress the minority arises. In reality, in a developed liberal democracy this does not necessarily happen: politicians operate with a sense of justice, and in framing legislation elected representatives often ignore the majority of their electorate, and pass laws protective of minority groups. A realistic model of the legislator is a person who is cross-pressured: he needs to get elected and re-elected and so cannot ignore the often illiberal views of the electorate, but at the same time he is moved by institutionally embodied principles of justice.

It is at the fourth – judicial – stage that Rawls thinks we have complete knowledge of the facts. This stage entails the application of rules, or laws, to particular cases by judges and administrators, and the following of rules by citizens (Rawls 1972: 199–200). The possibility of injustice arises at this stage and therefore also the scope for civil disobedience. Given my criticism of Rawls's description of the third – legislative – stage it would simplify the discussion if we combined the third and fourth stages, and simply called it the legislative stage.

With this sequence of stages now in place we can return to the paradox of conflicting obligations. First, how can we have an obligation to obey unjust laws? At the first stage – the original position – we know that principles of justice must be embodied in a constitution, and constitutions provide the framework for law-making. We also know that people are in conflict with one another, and so laws will never be passed unanimously – there will always be winners and losers. What is required is a decision-making rule which is acceptable to all. It is highly unlikely that anything other than majoritarianism would be chosen in the constitutional convention. The danger is that the majority will sometimes pass unjust laws – laws that deny rights to minority groups. Therefore we have a conflict: on the one hand, the principle of majority rule is effectively endorsed from stage one, which is a standpoint of moral equality, and so of justice, but on the other, majority rule will sometimes generate unjust laws. If an individual felt entitled, and perhaps obliged to break every law he deemed unjust, majoritarian democracy would collapse, and in the process so would the possibility of a just society. The question, or challenge – 'What if everyone did that?' – can always reasonably be asked of someone engaged in civil disobedience.

Rawls argues that the original position argument only works if we assume we have a moral duty to create and uphold just institutions – this is a natural duty in the sense that it precedes the choice of particular principles of justice. Recall that we enter the original position not knowing what principles we will choose, but we are committed to respecting whatever principles are chosen. We do not choose principles but then refuse to live by them. The natural duty to create and uphold just institutions entails respecting the real difficulties of putting principles into practice, and so not disobeying every law you think is unjust. On the other hand, upholding justice also means resisting injustice.

Civil disobedience involves making a judgement not between just and unjust laws but between different types of unjust laws. One suggestion Rawls makes for determining the point at which civil disobedience is justified is the degree to which a *particular group* bears the burden of injustice. If a group finds itself habitually, rather than occasionally, the victim of injustice then there are grounds for civil disobedience (Rawls 1972: 375).

The role of civil disobedience

Given the fact that in a just society decisions will be made by majority vote – subject to many checks and balances – the possibility of civil disobedience only arises for Rawls in a democratic society:

> At what point does the duty to comply with laws enacted by a legislative majority (or with executive acts supported by such a majority) cease to be binding in view of the right to defend one's liberties and the duty to oppose injustice? This involves the nature and limits of majority rule. For this reason the problem of civil disobedience is a crucial test for any theory of the moral basis of democracy (Rawls 1972: 363).

The leading idea behind Rawls's theory of civil disobedience is that in breaking the law *the civilly disobedient are addressing, or appealing to, the sense of justice of the majority*. All the other points that Rawls makes about civil disobedience lead back to this idea.

Rawls sets out a number of conditions on civil disobedience. It may seem pedantic to list and discuss these features, but for Rawls the definition of civil disobedience is closely bound up with its justification. I began with an initial definition of civil disobedience as morally justified law-breaking, but for Rawls not just any moral reasons justify law-breaking. There is an important distinction between civil disobedience and conscientious refusal. Furthermore, civil disobedience must not be confused with legal protest on one side, or rebellion on the other. So keeping these concerns in mind, we can list eight features of civil disobedience:

1. *Injustice must be clear.* What is unjust is determined by the principles of justice. Of the two, breaches of the first principle – equal liberty – are likely to be much clearer than denial of the second – the difference principle. For example, to deny a class of adults the right to vote on grounds of their ethnic or religious identity would be a clear infraction of the first principle. It is not only a clear injustice, but its remedy – granting the equal right to vote – is easy to grasp. On the other hand, significant economic inequality is much less *obviously* unjust, and the solution to the claimed injustice is not apparent (Rawls 1972: 372–3).

2. *It must involve breaking the law, rather than simply testing it.* Some laws are broken in order to force a judicial judgement, but this does not constitute civil disobedience (Rawls 1972: 367). As we will see this might rule out classifying significant aspects of the struggle against segregation in the Southern States of the USA as civil disobedience: much of the efforts of the Civil Rights Movement was directed at getting the Federal Courts to strike down states' laws as unconstitutional.

3. *It need not involve breaking the law which is the object of civil disobedience.* Laws are broken in the process of engaging in civil disobedience, but they need not be the direct object of the civilly disobedient action (Rawls 1972: 364–5). For example, in order to protest against an unjust war, you might sit down in the middle of the road, thus violating traffic laws, but clearly it is not the traffic laws that are the target of the action.

4. *It must be a public act.* Civil disobedience is a communicative act – the majority is being given fair notice that a law is unjust (Rawls 1972: 366). The communicative act consists not simply in the transmission of information – that could be achieved through covert action – but in getting the majority to understand that the civilly disobedient are making an appeal. Indeed, there is a distinction between communicating something to the majority, and *appealing* to it.

5. *It must be non-violent and not constitute a threat.* The reasoning behind this is similar to that behind (4) – the civilly disobedient want the majority to change the law for the right reason, namely, because it is unjust and not because the majority fear the consequences of maintaining the law (Rawls 1972: 366). Rawls could be criticized for naivety: one group may be genuinely non-violent and non-threatening, but their actions could be unintentionally threatening insofar as they make the majority aware of the existence of other, less peaceful, groups. The shadow of Malcolm X (and the Nation of Islam) was always behind that of Martin Luther King, and Malcolm X was perceived, correctly or not, to be an advocate of violence. Furthermore, it is not obvious that *non-violent* obstruction undermines the appeal to a sense of justice, and most campaigns have involved the deliberate *inconveniencing* of the majority.

6. *The civilly disobedient accept the penalties for law-breaking.* Once again, the reasoning behind this point is that the civilly disobedient are appealing to, rather than threatening, the majority. Willingness to accept the penalties for law-breaking – that is, not resisting arrest – demonstrates sincerity (Rawls 1972: 366). Such behaviour may embarrass the majority, who must ask themselves whether they really want to punish clearly peace-loving people.

7. *Even if laws are seriously unjust, civil disobedience must not threaten the stability of the political system.* A situation might arise where there are a number of groups justifiably engaged in civil

disobedience, but the conjoint effects of their actions threaten the political order. In such a situation groups must show restraint. Although it is rather unrealistic, Rawls suggests that civilly disobedient groups could come to an agreement whereby groups take turns in engaging in civil disobedience (Rawls 1972: 374). He may have in mind the US in the 1960s, when there were both civil rights *and* anti-Vietnam War actions. One might, however, wonder whether a political system which provokes so much civil disobedience is 'partially' just rather than simply unjust.

8. *Civil disobedience takes place within 'fidelity to law'.* This underwrites the entire project of civil disobedience. The civilly disobedient do not seek to bring down the existing system, but rather strengthen it by removing injustice, such that the system will win the loyalty of all citizens (Rawls 1972: 366–7). In this sense the civilly disobedient demonstrate fidelity – or faithfulness – to the law.

A distinction can be made between disobedience on general moral grounds, and disobedience on the narrower – but still moral – ground of injustice. Rawls's aim in *A Theory of Justice* was to articulate a morality – a theory of justice – appropriate to the political sphere. That political morality leaves open many other areas of morality. Conscientious refusal may be in harmony with political morality, but it need not be. It may be based on 'religious or other principles at variance with the constitutional order' (Rawls 1972: 369). The clearest modern example of conscientious refusal is objection to military service, either for general pacifist reasons, or because of opposition to a particular war. Rawls argues that such objections cannot *automatically* be accepted, for justice requires on occasion that people be prepared to defend – by force of arms – the political system (Rawls 1972: 370–1). However, he concedes that the spirit of pacifism accords with the values underlying a just society – it is rare for nearly just societies to go to war against one another.* He also argues that an unjust war – a war that violates the law of peoples – can quite properly be the object of civil disobedience.

Conscientious refusal is not, in itself, an appeal to the sense of justice of the majority, although it may be compatible with it: we could say that reasons grounded in religious and other non-political convictions may conform to political morality, but are not motivated by that morality. The danger with conscientious refusal is that it undermines the political order by substituting individual moral judgement for the collective judgement of society. An example would be the refusal to pay taxes that go towards the development and maintenance of nuclear weapons. It is possible that most people are nuclear pacifists – while they believe the use of conventional weapons can be justified, the employment of nuclear warheads represents a hugely disproportionate response to the aggression of another country. But among nuclear pacifists a majority might judge the *threat* to use – rather than actual use of – nuclear weapons is preferable to submission to a foreign power. Of course, a nuclear power has to convince the putative enemy country that it really will use weapons, and so there is an element of subterfuge, as well as risk, behind deterrence theory that seems at odds with the transparency one expects of a just society. Nonetheless, there can be reasonable disagreement regarding the morality of threatening to use nuclear weapons, such that the dissenting minority do not have grounds for civil disobedience. A final point to make regarding the distinction between civil disobedience and conscientious refusal is that the latter may entail a greater introversion than the former. A significant strand in conscientious refusal is the striving for moral integrity, that is, a feeling that *regardless of the consequences* you cannot support a law or policy. Insofar as conscientious refusal is a form of moral purity,

---

* This is the so-called 'democratic peace argument', which I discuss in Chapter 9.

it is in tension with civil disobedience, which looks outwards towards the majority, and appeals to it to change.

King and the civil rights movement

In this section I consider the arguments for civil disobedience advanced by Martin Luther King in his 'Letter from Birmingham City Jail', and assess the extent to which Rawls's conditions for civil disobedience hold for the Civil Rights Movement. Although Rawls rarely discusses contemporary political events in his work, it is clear that the Civil Rights Movement was a major influence on the development of his theory of civil disobedience (Rawls 1972: 364*n*), and it provides a valuable test case for it. King's Letter was addressed to fellow – mainly southern white – clergymen, some of whom had criticized King's campaign of civil disobedience. Given that Rawls argues civil disobedience is an appeal to the majority, it is important to recognize the *two* audiences King addresses: the clergy are the explicit addressees, but the majority of American citizens are the implicit addressees. Although he does not separate them out we can discern both Christian and secular arguments in the Letter. Of course, the great majority of Americans define themselves as Christian, but King communicates awareness that Christian arguments are not sufficient to justify civil disobedience. In setting out King's argument I follow his narrative of events. Obviously, his account should not be treated uncritically, but since my prime concern is with how he justified his actions from his perspective, and the relationship of his argument to that of Rawls, the veracity of the historical details can be left to historians. I assume some basic knowledge of the history of the Civil Rights Movement and only make reference to particular events in order to illustrate or criticize King's argument.

King sets out 'four basic steps' in a campaign of civil disobedience (King 11: 69): (a) the collection of facts to determine whether injustice is 'alive'; (b) negotiation; (c) self-purification; and (d) direct action. This fits with Rawls's emphasis on the communicative nature of civil disobedience – it is a last resort, taken only after other means of persuasion have failed. The actions which resulted in King's imprisonment – and the occasion for the letter – were illegal demonstrations in Birmingham, Alabama. These were directed against the 'whites only' and 'no coloreds' signs on shops, the segregated restaurants (lunch counters) and the deliberate negligence of the police to investigate eighteen bombings of black homes and churches over the previous six years. With regard to the first step, there was little doubt that Birmingham had one of the worst records on civil rights in the south.

The next step was to negotiate before engaging in civil disobedience. There were attempts to get the shopkeepers to remove their signs. Promises were made but not honoured. A Mayoral election in March 1963 between the reactionary Bull Connor and moderate – but still segregationist – Albert Boutwell resulted in the latter's victory, but because the three-man commission that had run Birmingham, and included Connor, refused to stand down, there was no movement on removal of discrimination. Negotiation had failed. The next step was self-purification. This must be distinguished from the introversion that characterizes conscientious refusal. The aim of self-purification is to ascertain whether the protestors will be able to endure violence without reacting violently. To this end, workshops on non-violent protest were held.

Finally, we come to the act of civil disobedience. King argues that one of the aims of civil disobedience is to 'create such a crisis and establish such creative tension that a community that has constantly refused to negotiate is forced to confront the issue' (King 1991: 71). The new Mayor Boutwell might be persuaded that resistance to desegregation was futile. It could be argued – and King was aware of this – that the effectiveness of civil disobedience rests on the existence of a violent alternative to it.

Those engaged in civil disobedience need not intend to communicate this message for this message to be communicated through their actions. In 1963 the widely perceived alternative to King was Malcolm X's Muslim movement. Indeed, King cites this movement in his letter, arguing that if civil rights activists are dismissed as 'rabble-rousers' and 'outside agitators' then millions of blacks 'out of frustration and despair, will seek solace and security in black nationalist ideologies, a development that will lead inevitably to a frightening racial nightmare' (King 1991: 77).

Responding to the question how it is possible to obey some laws but disobey others, King argues there are just laws and unjust laws:

> … an unjust law is a human law that is not rooted in eternal and natural law. Any law that uplifts human personality is just. Any law that degrades human personality is unjust. All segregation statutes are unjust because segregation distorts the soul and damages the personality. It gives the segregator a false sense of superiority, and the segregated a false sense of inferiority (King 1991: 73).

In expanding on this distinction King cites the Christian church fathers Augustine (354–430) and Aquinas (1225–74), Jewish philosopher Martin Buber (1878–1965) and Protestant theologian Paul Tillich (1886–1965). It may appear that King is appealing to a particular moral conception, drawn from Judaism and Christianity, rather than a *political* morality. Three points should be made. First, so long as the underlying appeal extends beyond your own particular conception of what is ultimately valuable, which for King is rooted in Christian teaching, then enlisting Christian (and Jewish) thinkers – Augustine, Aquinas, Buber, Tillich – is legitimate. In effect, King is saying 'I am a Christian, but you do not have to be a Christian to recognize the injustice I describe'. Insofar as we interpret King's argument for civil disobedience to be based on his

Christian beliefs it might be thought he is engaged in what Rawls terms conscientious refusal, but conscientious refusal is not incompatible with civil disobedience – a person, such as King, can be motivated by a secular political morality *and* a Christian morality. What would be problematic is an appeal only to a non-political morality. Second, the letter was written to Christian clergy, so the Christian references are unsurprising. Third, King goes on to re-state the argument in secular language:

> An unjust law is a code that a majority inflicts on a minority that is not binding on itself. This is difference made legal. On the other hand a just law is a code that a majority compels a minority to follow that it is willing to follow itself. This is sameness made legal (King 1991: 74).

He gives two examples, the first of which is problematic. Because the State of Alabama had denied blacks the right to vote they could not be bound by its laws. The danger with this argument is that even if blacks had voted, being in a minority they might have been subject to discriminatory laws. A rather better example is the denial of police permits to demonstrate: King accepts there should be controls on demonstrations, but objects to the misuse of permits to deny civil rights activists the possibility of peaceful protest, while opponents of civil rights can protest unhindered (King 1991: 74).

King argues that a sign of the good faith of the civil rights activists is that they break the law openly and are willing to accept the penalties for law-breaking. These are of course on Rawls's list of conditions for civil disobedience. And finally, as if to underline the stabilizing power of civil disobedience, King concludes his letter with the following statement:

> One day the South will know that when the disinherited children of God sat down at lunch counters they were in reality

standing up for the best in the American dream and the most sacred values in our Judeo-Christian heritage, and thusly, carrying our whole nation back to those great wells of democracy which were dug deep by the founding fathers in the formulation of the Constitution and the Declaration of Independence (King 1991: 84).

What makes the Civil Rights Movement an important example of civil disobedience is that in philosophical terms it took place in the space between the constitution and lower-level law: in Rawls's language, between the constitutional and legislative stages. This may also, however, raise some definitional difficulties. The most visible aspect of the civil rights struggle was the clash between supporters and opponents of equal rights in the streets, on the buses and at the lunch counters. But behind that struggle was another: a struggle between federal law and constitutional judgements on the one side, and the southern states on the other. It is notable that when defenders of segregation organized themselves politically – at elections – they adopted the banner of States' Rights: the rights of the states against the President, Congress and the Supreme Court. Civil disobedience was made possible by: (a) the existence of a (basically) just constitution, and (b) the refusal at a lower level of law-making to respect the constitution. It could be argued that what the civil rights activists were doing was appealing not to the majority of fellow Americans, but to the judiciary. In effect, they were forcing test cases for the legitimacy of state law. On the other hand, it might be maintained that it was through elected representatives in Congress – representatives of 'the majority' – that the great strides forward in civil rights were made. But then the failure of the Civil Rights Movement to change Southerners' attitudes is revealed in the Congressional voting figures for the most important single piece of desegregation legislation, the Civil Rights Act (1964). In the Senate, the Democrats divided 46–21 in favour

(69% in favour) and the Republicans were 27–6 in favour (82%). All southern Democratic Senators voted against. In the House of Representatives, the Democrats divided 152–96 in favour (61%) and the Republicans 138–34 in favour (80%). Of the Southern Democratic Congressman 92 out of 103 (89%) voted against.

Punishment

Philosophical discussions of punishment tend to be dominated by two theories: retributivism and utilitarianism (or, more broadly, consequentialism). Retributivism is often characterized rather crudely as requiring that law-breakers should suffer in proportion to their crimes, whereas utilitarians (or consequentialists) look to the effects of the system of punishment on future behaviour, not only, or even primarily, on the behaviour of those who are punished, but on the behaviour of all citizens. Although retributivism looks crude, there is a powerful, if standard, objection to utilitarianism: it justifies the punishment of the innocent – that is, those who have not committed the act(s) to which the punishment is in some sense connected. The intuition that only the guilty should be punished is very strong. Yet there is also a sense that punishment should serve a purpose, and if it does not then suffering is being inflicted without reason.

What Rawls seeks to do in 'Two Concepts of Rules' is develop a theory of punishment that reconciles these two intuitions: that only the guilty should be punished, but also that punishment should serve a purpose. The essay ranges more widely than punishment: it discusses promise-keeping, and locates both punishment and promise-keeping within a framework of rule-following.

The key to reconciling our apparently conflicting intuitions is to distinguish the justification of a 'practice' as a *system of rules*, and justifying *actions* carried out through those rules (Rawls 1999b: 22). Utilitarian arguments apply to the practice and not to the actions. To illustrate further the distinction, Rawls defines two positions: the legislator and the judge. The legislator determines the rules, and thus the purpose of punishment, whereas the judge applies those rules to particular cases. The rules specify that a person who commits a particular act will be treated in a particular way, and the judge simply applies those rules without considering the wider purpose of punishment (Rawls 1999b: 23). Rawls's argument anticipates later developments in utilitarian thought away from what is sometimes called act-utilitarianism (or direct utilitarianism) towards rule-utilitarianism and institutional utilitarianism (these are forms of indirect utilitarianism). The leading idea behind indirect utilitarianism is that the maximization of utility is best achieved if we desist from trying *on each occasion* to maximize utility. Rather, we follow rules or respect institutions, the operation of which will, *over time*, maximize utility. Some writers have argued that rule-utilitarianism would, if we had perfect knowledge, be extensionally equivalent to act-utilitarianism, for we would be able to calculate when a departure from the rules would maximize utility (Lyons 1965: 137–43). The implication of Rawls's argument is that under conditions of imperfect knowledge, it is much safer to respect institutions. To illustrate the point he asks the reader to imagine an institution which he calls 'telishment', that allows for the punishment of an innocent person whenever the officials empowered by that institution judge that, by deterring crime, it will maximize utility (Rawls 1999b: 27). It will achieve that end only if the general public believe that he committed the offence for which he is being 'telished': if they believe there is no connection between offence and 'punishment' (or telishment), then the institution of telishment will be ineffective. Rawls's point is that such an *institution* would require an impossible level of conspiracy and deception.

There is, however, a fundamental problem with Rawls's argument. We can distinguish the offices of legislator and judge, but political philosophy aims to provide a comprehensive justification for political principles and institutions. There must, therefore, be a standpoint from which we can understand the reasons why we punish people, and that standpoint must incorporate the reasoning of both legislator and judge. In other words, these two officers are metaphors for a division within the moral psychology of the citizen and not descriptions of real people within political institutions. For citizens to *believe* that punishment is fundamentally connected to personal responsibility, such that only the guilty ought to be punished, they must be denied knowledge of the utilitarian justification for the institution. In short, citizens can only think like judges and not legislators. This restriction is incompatible with one of the conditions of formal right, namely publicity, and resembles what Bernard Williams dubbed 'Government House Utilitarianism', where an elite understand the purpose of the institution, but for reasons of stability must deny the masses access to that understanding (Williams 1985: 108–10).

Rawls's argument can, however, be saved from this objection but only by recasting it as non–utilitarian and connecting it to his later, more developed theory of justice. If you recall the discussion of the prisoner's dilemma in Chapter 2, coercion (or the threat of coercion) is necessary to assure one another that an agreement to submit to a state (or set of political institutions) is rational. It follows that an institution of punishment must be established. This argument leaves open the possibility of telishment, for we only need to *believe* the guilty will be punished. And there is nothing in the logic of a resolution to the prisoner's dilemma that requires publicity – 'Government House' can supply the assurance which rational agents seek. As such, the prisoner's dilemma suggests a consequentialist justification for punishment: it must serve the end of social order. However, I argued that the agreement to submit to an authority as a means of resolving the prisoner's dilemma was only the beginning for a theory of justice: we need a moral resolution to the dilemma, and morality has formal features, such as publicity.

Institutions must be justified to *all* who are subject to them, such that nobody would will that he be punished for a crime which he had not committed, and, by extension, we could not agree to telishment. And this is a much stronger argument against telishment than the one advanced by Rawls: telishment is not merely inefficient or unstable, but excluded by the nature of the moral choice procedure.

Interestingly, in his discussion of rules towards the end of his essay, Rawls offers the basis of this argument. The 'two concepts of rules' alluded to in the title of the essay are (a) rules of thumb derived from the recurrence of similar cases, and (b) rules that define a practice in which cases are judged (Rawls 1999b: 34–5). The weaker objection against telishment – that it would not work – relies on the idea that experience teaches us it is better to punish the guilty and not the innocent (type (a) rules). The stronger objection to telishment – that the rules directly preclude it – depends on the justification of political institutions being logically prior to the operation of those institutions (type (b) rules). The second, practice-based, concept of rules anticipates the development of the original position in which autonomous moral agents determine principles of justice – both distributive, and although not discussed by Rawls, retributive – to which *each and every* agent can agree under conditions of fairness.

Further reading

The only book-length treatment of Rawls's theory of civil disobedience is Haksar (1986). Barry (1973), Chapters 13–14, deals with the just constitution (relevant to the four-stage sequence). There is a good essay on civil disobedience by Feinberg in Richardson and Weithman (1999; vol. 1). See also Kukathas (2003; vol. 2), part 10 (civil disobedience). For a discussion of punishment (more, specifically, the two concepts of rules) see essays by Margolis and McCloskey in Richardson and Weithman (1999; vol. 1).

8
Political liberalism

In the 1980s Rawls began to revise the account of justice which he had presented in his earlier work. Largely unchanged were the substantive principles, but in a series of articles, culminating in the book *Political Liberalism* (Rawls 1996),★ he revised the justificatory basis of the theory. He had assumed that in a well-ordered society there was a widely, and deeply, shared moral code. But this belief does not, he now suggests, address the 'fact' of 'reasonable pluralism': the existence of conflicting, yet reasonably held, conceptions of the good. He does not abandon the idea of the original position but his interpretation of it undergoes a significant change.

Rawls's shift is sometimes explained as a response to the challenge of multiculturalism – a challenge which was not strongly articulated in the early post-war decades when *A Theory of Justice* was being written. Much of the multiculturalism debate is concerned with institutional questions, such as making national symbols more culturally inclusive, ensuring that employment

★ All references are to the 1996 paperback edition of *Political Liberalism*. The book was originally published in 1993, but the 1996 edition has an interesting additional Preface and includes as the last 'Lecture' (or chapter) Rawls's response to Habermas. I discuss the Rawls–Habermas debate in the last section of this chapter.

law reflects the diversity of the workforce and funding of faith schools. Rawls's late work, while relevant to these public policy issues, addresses more fundamental philosophical questions about human agency in a religiously and culturally diverse society.

A moralized *modus vivendi*

A central point of *Political Liberalism*, as indicated by its title, is that a theory of justice must be *political*, meaning its motivational force must derive from a particular, circumscribed, sphere of life, and not from a comprehensive moral standpoint. This is a radical claim: it is not a reprise of the standard liberal argument for the distinction between public and private, whereby individuals enjoy a sphere of freedom in which they can act in ways that others might reasonably disapprove of, but rather, the claim is that the basis of justification is itself limited to the political. We can compare this with, for example, John Stuart Mill's political theory. Mill defended the public/private distinction through the use of the harm principle but from a comprehensive moral standpoint, which was a complex form of utilitarianism. The argument for his harm principle entailed the *application* to the political sphere of a general moral conception. This, in Rawls's view, is sectarian, for one can be in reasonable disagreement with Mill's utilitarianism.

The distinction between a political and a comprehensive conception of the good in turn affects how we understand the motivational basis of Rawls's theory. It is important that this distinction is not defined in terms of the political *as opposed to* the 'moral', for the political conception is itself a moral conception, but a special one. Somehow, the agent must accept the principles of justice but for the right reasons, and that means as principles with independent moral force. How then the moral force of political principles can be restricted to the political sphere is a major challenge, and one Rawls does not satisfactorily resolve. He argues that the historical roots of political liberalism lie in the settlement of the Wars of Religion of the sixteenth and seventeenth centuries (Rawls 1996: xxv–xxvi), but the *modus vivendi* which was achieved became *moralized*: toleration of religious difference – even if in historical terms a mere compromise between opposing camps which could not destroy each other – gave rise to political principles with a motivational force independent of power relations.

Although Rawls makes no claim to be an historian of ideas, and his references to the history of religious toleration are quite sweeping, it is nonetheless useful to reflect briefly on the historical roots of toleration. Although the term 'Wars of Religion' is sometimes reserved for a series of civil wars fought in France between 1562 and 1598, the term can be used more widely to include the struggle of the Protestant Netherlands (United Provinces) to free themselves from Catholic Spain and the Thirty Years War (1618–48) in Germany. From the settlement of these wars it is claimed that a doctrine of toleration emerged that was given philosophical expression by, among others, Spinoza, Voltaire and Locke. Although to contemporary ears the word 'toleration' has slightly pejorative overtones, implying grudging acceptance rather than respect, it remains an important concept and we need to be clear about its structure.

Toleration appears paradoxical, for it seems to require simultaneous approval and disapproval of that which is tolerated. For example, an orthodox (Roman) Catholic will hold that salvation is only possible through communion with the Church (of Rome), and the relationship between human beings and God is mediated through a priesthood. A mainstream Protestant, on the other hand, will maintain that salvation requires an individual act, and while the Church plays an important ministering role, there is no special class of people – a priesthood – through whom we must go in order to achieve salvation. Toleration requires that Catholics and Protestants have rights to practice their religion, and furthermore, should not be denied other rights as a result of exercising their freedom of religion. Yet neither side can accept the truth or validity of the other's beliefs and actions. The paradox is that a Catholic must maintain there is no salvation outside the Church (of Rome), but also that a non-Catholic is justified in not seeking salvation through the Church.

We can start to resolve the paradox if we recognize that validity attaches to different actions – a Catholic cannot approve of a non-Catholic's choice, but can respect his or her *capacity* for choice. There is, nonetheless, still a tension, for both religions (or streams of Christianity) must attach value to the capacity for choice, or find some other element common to both. Historians of religious thought have identified many different common elements which have enabled mutual toleration. These have included the importance of Christian unity ('catholicism' in the generic sense of the word); the idea that God gave humans a choice, so that we should respect one another's choices, even if the result is damnation; and recognition that human beings will always be unsure of what God requires of us and so a degree of dissent is permissible (latitudinarianism). These are attempts to bridge religious differences through identification of a common ground, but there is another way of understanding toleration – an acceptance of political reality: terrible torture and other deprivations will not force (some) people to abandon their religious beliefs and practices, so it is both useless and politically destabilizing to oppress them. Such a view assumes there can be no common ground, or at least the common ground is not sufficiently firm to support political institutions. This is what is meant by a *modus vivendi* – literally, a 'way of living', but here implying a way of co-existing despite profound religious differences.

If we look at the *politics* of religious toleration, as distinct from later *philosophical discourse* on toleration, we see that *modus vivendi* arguments occupy a prominent place. Some old Protestant accounts of the Wars of Religion trace the roots of the conflict to the Church of Rome's attempt to suppress dissent. However, it is more accurate to attribute the conflict to the legitimation crisis caused for secular authorities by Protestants' institutional break with Rome. In states where the Prince (or Elector) had embraced Lutheranism or Calvinism, the continuing allegiance of some of his citizens to Rome was a threat to his authority. Conversely, where the Prince had remained loyal to Rome but some of his subjects had embraced Reformed religion, there was a loss of spiritual authority – an authority which had underwritten secular power in the pre-Reformation period. In addition, the mediaeval division of spiritual and secular power had resulted in a dual structure of law, with much domestic law – for example marriage – the responsibility of church courts, rather than secular courts. In Reformed states, the legitimacy of that domestic law was now in question.

The first Europe-wide attempt to address, rather than simply suppress, this conflict of loyalties, was the Treaty of Augsburg (1555), which produced the formula: *cujus regio, eius religio* – roughly translated as 'the ruler determines the religion'. Two points can be made about this formula. First, it tolerated rulers and not individual citizens. Second, it was a simple *modus vivendi* – it carried no underlying respect for the other person's beliefs or way of life. It was a recognition of the reality of power: neither side could destroy the other, and it was in neither's interest for there to be continual war, so they agreed to disagree. However, once the balance of power shifted, the newly dominant side had no reason not to suppress the other. Not surprisingly, the Augsburg settlement proved unstable, and it took a century more of conflict before the so-called Peace of Westphalia (1648) created a new, and relatively stable, European order. The Peace of Westphalia is the name given to a series of treaties which ended the last of the great wars of religion – the Thirty Years War (1618–48). It re-affirmed the formula of *cujus regio, eius religio*, but made some concession to the toleration of individuals by respecting the beliefs of those resident in a particular territory prior to 1618. Only gradually did moral theories based on the idea of toleration – or what Rawls terms a moralized *modus vivendi* – emerge. The task for Rawls is to explain how an historical account can generate a moral theory, that is, how a mere *modus vivendi* became a moralized one.

Stability

Rawls argues that *A Theory of Justice* relied on a premise the realization of which is ruled out by the principles of justice: 'that in the well-ordered society of justice as fairness, citizens hold the same comprehensive doctrine, and this includes aspects of Kant's comprehensive liberalism, to which the principles of justice might belong' (Rawls 1996: xlii). The argument seems to be that the liberty of conscience contained in the principles of justice conflicts with the supposed derivation of that liberty from a comprehensive, Kantian liberalism. The theory is, as it stands, unstable, and so what is required is a transformation of the comprehensive aspects of justice as fairness into political doctrines. This apparent contradiction between the substantive principles of justice and their derivation can be interpreted in two different ways. It might be a logical incoherence: if tolerance is required at the substantive level of political principle then it must also apply to the methodological level – that is, the way we justify principles. Alternatively, it could be an empirical observation that unless liberty of conscience, and other rights, are derived in the right way – in a way that recognizes reasonable disagreement over comprehensive conceptions of the good – then outside the original position the principles of justice will not command sufficient respect. Both these arguments are present in *Political Liberalism*, but the latter argument has greater prominence.

A well-ordered society, Rawls argued, is regulated by a public conception of justice, and 'this fact implies that its members have a strong and normally effective desire to act as the principles of justice require' (Rawls 1972: 454). Since a well-ordered society endures over time we can assume its conception of justice is stable, meaning that citizens acquire 'the corresponding sense of justice and desire to do their part in maintaining them' (Rawls 1972: 454). One particular conception of justice is more stable than another the more effective it is in engendering a sense of justice. Rawls's aim in *A Theory of Justice* is to show that for this reason his preferred 'democratic conception' is more stable than the alternatives, such as utilitarianism, intuitionism or perfectionism. It is important to stress that Rawls's theory is not a proposal to be accepted or rejected, but is an attempt to describe our rational psychology. This is important in our understanding of stability: the original position should provide the necessary motivation on the Kantian principle of ought implies can, such that stability provides no additional motivation.

Stability is best seen as part of a reflexive process whereby agents in the original position test putative principles of justice for their long-term success in engendering a sense of justice in *real* citizens. Rawls assumes agents in the original person have a sense of justice, meaning they are prepared to live by principles which they have freely chosen. If, however, outside the original position we find it difficult to live by principles – perhaps because they require too great a sacrifice of our interests or are in serious tension with our conceptions of the good – then that instability should force us back to the original position. Rawls makes it clear in *A Theory of Justice* that stability is not an add on to the motivation generated by the original position but is a way of testing competing principles of justice. The problem of stability may, however, force us back not to a reconsideration of what is chosen in the original position, but to its very construction. In *Political Liberalism* Rawls retains much of the terminology of his earlier work – the original position, veil of ignorance, conception of the person and so on – but reinterprets them.

In large part, this reinterpretation stems from a new under-standing of the problem of stability, one that is sociological rather than psychological. In reinterpreting the problem of stability Rawls alters the *rational psychology* presented in *A Theory of Justice*. Because of the deep pluralism that exists in society, personal autonomy ceases to be intrinsic to the construction of political principles but is expressed only in the content of those prin-ciples. Instead of the motivation to endorse and act upon prin-ciples of justice flowing from the comprehensive standpoint of autonomous choice, motivation has two sources: each person's comprehensive doctrine and the political conception. It is, in Rawls's view, unreasonable to expect that everybody be moti-vated to accept the principles of justice from the standpoint of the comprehensive value of autonomy. The challenge for Rawls is to explain how human beings reconcile reasons derived from these different sources.

One way of reconciling these reasons would be to accept there exist separate spheres of validity, such as a sphere of secu-lar, political values and a sphere of spiritual, theological values. Even if we accept religious toleration grew out of the fact of pluralism, its moralization depended on a conception of ratio-nality that both institutionalized the spheres of validity and transcended them. Institutionalization would entail develop-ing a set of political principles, such as rights to freedom of worship and open access to public office. Transcendence is a corresponding explanation of how theological principles can be dominant within their own sphere, but subordinate to secular principles in the political sphere. In short, we need an account of how the secular and the theological fit together. The diffi-culty with ignoring the question of how the spheres of validity fit together is that we have no explanation for how a simple *modus vivendi* became moralized, or even whether it is coher-ent to talk of a *moralized modus vivendi*. Rawls does argue that 'this pluralism is not seen as a disaster but rather as the natural outcome of the activities of human reason under enduring free institutions. To see reasonable pluralism as a disaster is to see the exercise of reason under the conditions of freedom itself as a disaster' (Rawls 1996: xxvi–xxvii). But this assumes the reasonable comprehensive conceptions of the good have the kind of structure such that they would emerge under conditions of freedom. Religious fundamentalism, for example, emerged under conditions of modernity, but it has a structure that is resistant to the liberal freedoms which Rawls claims are also the product of modernity. The fact that under modernity there are generated divergent belief-systems – liberal and illiberal – does not invalidate Rawls's observation that modern liberal-democratic societies have produced a public sphere in which a plurality of beliefs is accepted. However, the basic point remains that a historical account is inadequate – we need a philosophical account of the structure of a *reasonable* comprehensive conception of the good, and, by extension, of reasonable pluralism.

Reasonable pluralism

Rawls argues that in his earlier theory he did not fully recognize the 'fact of pluralism'. Given the references to religious toleration and the idea of a *modus vivendi* it is possible to present this 'fact' as simply the brute reality of difference. Rawls, however, defines it as the existence of conflicting, yet *reasonably held*, comprehensive conceptions of the good (Rawls 1996: xviii). But he offers two competing accounts of reasonable disagreement. He does not present them as separate accounts, but in my view they are both separate and in tension with one another. First, we have the burdens of judgement – 'the many hazards involved in the correct (and conscientious) exercise of our powers of reason and judgement in the ordinary course of political life' (Rawls 1996: 56):

1. The evidence – empirical and scientific – bearing on the case is conflicting and complex, and thus hard to assess and evaluate.
2. Even if we agree fully about the kinds of considerations that are relevant, we may disagree about their weight, and so arrive at different judgements.
3. To some extent all our concepts, and not only moral and political concepts, are vague and subject to hard cases.
4. To some extent (how great we cannot tell) the way we assess evidence and weigh moral and political values is shaped by our total experience, our whole course of life up to now, and our total experience must always differ.
5. Often there are different kinds of normative considerations of different force on both sides of an issue and it is difficult to make an overall assessment. (There may be a conflict between perspectives that specify obligations, rights, utility, perfectionist ends and personal commitments.)
6. Any system of social institutions is limited in the values it can admit so that some selection must be made from the full range of moral and political values that might be realized (Rawls 1996: 56–7).

What is striking about this list is it assumes individuals share a great deal: they are engaged in a debate. A parallel can be drawn between the burdens of judgement and Jürgen Habermas's notion of communicative action. Habermas, whose work has important parallels with Rawls's and is discussed in the last section of this chapter, argues that in addressing another person I raise a validity claim (or claims) which must be 'redeemed'. If, for example, I were to argue that the distribution of resources should take account of labour expended, and that some people *deserve* more resources because they have worked harder – an argument Rawls rejects – then I raise a validity claim: in effect, I am proposing to others that desert is morally relevant in the distribution of resources and other people can challenge such a claim. Rawls's burdens of judgement imply a Habermasian raising of validity claims. Because Rawls expresses the burdens in negative form the parallel with the positive Habermasian conception of validity-claims is obscured. It is nonetheless present: to say a reasonable person recognizes evidence is conflicting and complex, or that various weights can be attached to different considerations, or that our concepts are 'vague and subject to hard cases', or that conflicts exist between different kinds of moral principles or that no social world can contain a full range of values is to adopt a standpoint in which the force of different arguments can be recognized from *within* the rational psychology of the agent.

The idea of reasonable disagreement as the raising of validity-claims conflicts with the next step in Rawls's argument, which is to define a reasonable comprehensive conception of the good:

1. It entails the exercise of theoretical reason.
2. It entails the exercise of practical reason.
3. 'While a reasonable comprehensive view is not necessarily fixed and unchanging, it normally belongs to, or draws upon, a tradition of thought and doctrine' (Rawls 1996: 59). It is not subject to 'sudden and unexplained changes, it tends to evolve slowly in the light of what, *from its point of view*, it sees as good and sufficient conditions' (Rawls 1996: 59, emphasis added).

Rawls is careful to hedge this final point with qualifications, recognizing that otherwise it would be 'arbitrary and exclusive': 'we avoid excluding doctrines as unreasonable without strong grounds based on clear aspects of the reasonable itself' (Rawls 1996: 59). The problem is the burdens of judgement are in tension with his account of reasonable doctrines. The burdens imply agents are engaged in a dispute in which there is considerable tacit agreement: we are not faced with people whose views of the world are mutually incomprehensible, for if they were they would not be able to recognize and accept conflict and complexity. The doctrines, on the other hand, differ in at least two ways. Whereas with regard to the burdens Rawls leaves it open as to whether the dispute applies to quite specific problems, or general world-views, the doctrines imply a comprehensive view of the world, entailing both theoretical and practical judgements. The other difference is that while the burdens define the dispute in non-historical terms, the doctrines make reference to a tradition. There is no necessary point of contact between traditions, so the conflict does not imply that the different positions are engaged in a debate. Whereas the burdens presuppose a conception of reason, the doctrines are *historical*. Put crudely, it seems to count in favour of the reasonableness of a doctrine that it has been around a long time.

Although it is difficult to reconcile the ideas of a critical reasonable pluralism (akin to Habermas's validity-claims) and an uncritical acceptance of tradition, it is clear that Rawls does intend to affect a reconciliation. We need to introduce a further concept to explain how a person can be motivated by his tradition – for example, his religious beliefs – and yet political principles can be free-standing and derived from a moral choice situation in which people are denied knowledge of their religious beliefs. This new concept is the 'overlapping consensus'.

Overlapping consensus

The overlapping consensus assumes there are two motivational bases for the principles of justice. The political – the 'great values of liberalism' – is 'free standing' (Rawls 1996: 10), meaning the political should directly motivate the individual. But it is left to citizens as part of their liberty of conscience individually to work out how those values relate to their own comprehensive conceptions. The idea is that reasonable comprehensive doctrines endorse the political conception, *each from its own point of view*. Given that what we are justifying is the application of coercive power, it needs to be shown that each person can affirm his comprehensive doctrine and yet hold it would not be reasonable to use state power to gain everyone's allegiance to it. The problem is that the appeal to liberty of conscience is circular: it is precisely the political principles which stand in need of justification, such that they cannot themselves be part of the justification process. Some commentators are untroubled by this circularity, arguing that only liberals will be liberal (Barry 1990: 11). However, this is to abandon criticism in favour of an appeal to the unifying force of pre-reflective sentiments – it is tautologically true that only liberals will be liberal, but the reasons we give to people, including to ourselves, must extend beyond the phenomenology of those beliefs. If somebody says 'I do not endorse liberal principles because I am not a liberal', then what can we say? If there is nothing we can say – if we can give no reasons for endorsing those principles – it is hard to claim we are being reasonable. If we *can* say something then it follows that political values have a persuasive force independent of any particular comprehensive conceptions of the good.

The overlapping consensus can be interpreted either as beginning with political values, and then the individual attempts to fit those values into his comprehensive conception of the good, or the individual moves towards the political values from his own comprehensive conception of the good. Of course it may be argued that we do both: we move, as it were, back and forth between the political and comprehensive conceptions. But the stability of Rawls's theory of justice depends upon there being an affinity between the political and the comprehensive. The overlap cannot be contingent. The conflict within the rational psychology of the agent between the political and the comprehensive reflects, in my view, the conflict in Rawls's definition of reasonable disagreement between the burdens of judgement and the appeal to tradition.

Rawls offers no sustained demonstration of how an overlapping consensus functions, and so it would be useful to provide an example in order to test his thesis. I will take the case of Muslim allegiance to the two principles of justice as a test-case for Rawls's revised theory. There are two dimensions to the test: can Muslims be motivated to respect the two principles? And can they do so for the 'right reasons'? Achieving agreement for the right reasons would entail the political – the 'great values of liberalism' – directly motivating Muslims, but in a way that fitted with their religious and associated cultural values. The political has to fit like a 'module' into their comprehensive conception of the good (Rawls 1996: 12–13). We can list a number of features of Muslim belief which may be problematic, alongside what might be termed justice-consistent interpretations of those features:

1. In classical Islamic jurisprudence the world is divided into *dar-al-Islam* (realm of Islam) and *dar-al-Harb* (realm of war, which equates to the non-Muslim areas of the world opposed to Islam). This distinction may suggest an inability to tolerate non-Muslims, but, in fact, many historians claim that Islam has a long history of toleration of Jews and Christians, grounded in the belief that Islam is an aboriginal and natural form of monotheism, and incorporates the Prophets of the Jews and the Christians. While the term *dar-al-Islam* refers to a geographical area in which holy law (*Shariah*) is most effective, most classical theorists did not regard this distinction as a reason to wage war against *dar-al-Harb* but rather to conduct active missionary work. There is a third realm – *dar-al-Sulh* – where mutual recognition of Muslims and non-Muslims holds, and which may be an appropriate description of a liberal society.

2. _Shariah_ (holy law) encompasses all aspects of life and so cannot respect the private sphere, and the liberal idea of the 'right to do wrong'. However, so long as secular law is not incompatible with _Shariah_, then the former should be obeyed, and there are arguments in Islam for obeying secular rulers. It may also be argued that _Shariah_ only applies in _dar-al-Islam_ and a lesser requirement holds in _dar-al-Sulh_, namely that secular law should not render it impossible for Muslims to practice their faith.

3. _Jihad_ (exertion, struggle) may imply intolerance of non-Muslims and enjoin Muslims to engage in armed struggle against them. However, it should be noted that a believer is required to carry out _jihad_ by 'his heart; his tongue; his hands; and by the sword', so _jihad_ can be interpreted as an individual, spiritual struggle.

4. 'Islam' is often defined as 'submission' or 'self-surrender' – this appears incompatible with respect for human autonomy, and, by extension makes impossible the justification of principles of justice from a standpoint of moral autonomy (the original position). However, submission understood as _self-imposed discipline_ is not incompatible with respect for human freedom; a person might _choose_ to submit.

5. For Muslims, behaviour is classified as: (a) required – this includes prayer, alms-giving, fasting; (b) prohibited – theft, illicit sex, alcohol consumption; (c) recommended – charitable acts, additional prayers and fasts; (d) discouraged – this might include unilateral declarations of divorce by men; (e) morally indifferent. From the perspective of respect for secular law (b) raises difficulties – while the interpretation of 'theft' depends on the definition of property, the other prohibited actions are certainly 'permitted' under the principles of justice. The liberal response is to appeal to the distinction between public and private and maintain that public permission does not require private approval, and so long as

Muslims do not violate individuals' rights they can impose sanctions on prohibited behaviour.

6. There are requirements on women to cover themselves – to hide their 'adornments', meaning their own physical beauty and such things as jewellery. The requirements seem to be gender-specific and imply inequality, especially when combined with other restrictions. However, the requirement on women to cover themselves can be interpreted as symbolic – in the Arab-Islamic world there is huge variation in what is required of women. Modesty is also expected of men.

Each of these points can be contested, but it is at least plausible to argue Muslims can be *politically* liberal. Other citizens – Christians, Jews, Hindus, atheists and so – will, of course, produce different lists of reasons for endorsing liberal principles. In that sense, principles of justice will be stable, but Rawls insists he is offering stability for the right reasons. I would interpret this as requiring a form of justification that goes deeper than the contingent overlap between conceptions of the good. Certainly, empirical evidence would suggest that Muslims living in Western, liberal societies can, over time, acquire values similar to those of the majority community. But mere empirical convergence does not guarantee long-term stability. To address this second question requires a further exploration of the relationship between political liberalism and comprehensive conceptions of the good, and a useful way of doing this is to compare the work of Rawls and Habermas.

Rawls and Habermas

Habermas, who was born in 1929, is the best-known contemporary German philosopher, and his work is often compared to

Rawls's, in part because both draw on the Kantian tradition. In 1995 the two thinkers engaged in a debate in the pages of the *Journal of Philosophy*, with Habermas advancing a critique of Rawls's idea of public reason (Habermas 1995). Rawls's response was reproduced in the paperback edition of *Political Liberalism*. To understand and assess the differences between the two thinkers it is necessary to give a brief outline of Habermas's rather complex social and political theory.

Habermas defends the emancipatory potential of the Enlightenment against thinkers who argue, along with Max Weber, that Western society is characterized by an increasing instrumentalization of reason. This instrumentalization – what Habermas calls systemic rationality – threatens traditional forms of life, including religious beliefs. Against systemic rationality Habermas reconstructs another form of rationality implicit in everyday life: communicative rationality (which then forms the basis of a 'discourse ethics'). People engage in speech–acts: person A *promises* to meet person B on Thursday, *requests* B stop smoking, *confesses* to find B's actions distasteful, *predicts* it will rain. Implicit in each speech–act is an offer, which B can contest. In the first two cases A is making a claim to normative rightness, in the third case a claim to sincerity, and in the final case a claim to truth. B can contest all three such claims (Habermas 1984: 295–6). The success of each speech–act depends upon both parties orienting themselves to principles of reason which, unlike systemic action, are not reducible to individuals' instrumental, self-interested intentions: in addressing B person A treats him as an end-in-himself. The validity–claims are implicit in all human action – they are universal. However, the validity–claims abstract from everyday life – culture or religion – and so to redeem them, meaning to come to an agreement about what is right or wrong, requires appeal to a stock of culturally specific values.

One way to address this problem of culture-dependence is to maintain that politics is a dialogue, in which people bring to bear their different cultural perspectives, so that what emerges from the dialogue is something pluralistic yet coherent. For example, Muslims might be criticized by Western feminists for projecting a patriarchal conception of gender relations. By engaging in dialogue Muslims may reform their view of women's rights, but Westerners might also be obliged to recognize the deficiencies in their own understanding of sexual relations by, for example, acknowledging the costs entailed in the commodification of sex in a liberal society.

This dialogical approach to politics Habermas contrasts with the Anglophone tradition in legal and political theory that conceptualizes the state as grounded in the protection of individual 'private' rights – rights derived from the market contract model. Hobbes is the *locus classicus* of this conception of individual-state relations. If we operate with such a theory then it is inevitable that individual rights, such as those contained in Rawls's first principle of justice, will be a threat to religious forms of life. For example, rights tend to privatize religious experience – attending church becomes another choice, like buying a new pair of shoes. In effect, increasing reliance on rights would be another example of systemic rationality eroding the 'lifeworld' – that is, taken-for-granted forms of life. We are then left with a choice: either we assert the primacy of individual rights at the expense of cultural interaction, or we maintain the oppressive authority of the collective over the individual. Habermas seeks to defend liberal rights, but in a way sensitive to cultural attachments. He argues that while private rights entail the assertion of personal autonomy, they ignore the other half of the concept of autonomy – public autonomy:

> … from a normative point of view, the integrity of the individual legal person cannot be guaranteed without protecting the intersubjectively shared experiences and life contexts in which the person has been socialized and has formed his or her

> identity. The identity of the individual is interwoven with collec-
> tive identities and can be stabilized only in a cultural network
> that cannot be appropriated as private property any more than
> the mother tongue itself can be (Habermas 1994: 129).

The implication of Habermas's argument is that principles of
justice are, contrary to Rawls's theory, grounded in human
autonomy, but that human autonomy itself has a collective
dimension that must take into account cultural interpretations
of those principles.

Rawls claims that Habermas is offering a comprehensive
account of justice, whereas Rawls's own (late) theory is limited
to the political. Rawls argues that 'political liberalism moves
within the category of the political and leaves philosophy as it is
… it leaves untouched all kinds of doctrines – religious, metaphysical, and moral – with their long traditions of development
and interpretation' (Rawls 1996: 375). What is at stake in the
debate between Rawls and Habermas is the nature of justification: can we justify political principles in a way that does not
presuppose controversial beliefs incompatible with respect for
reasonable comprehensive conceptions? For Habermas, justification is discursive: we raise and settle validity-claims, and in the
process come to form a common good. Rawls, on the other hand,
distinguishes three types of justification: *pro tanto* justification of
the political conception; full justification of that conception by
an individual person in society; and finally, public justification
of the political conception by political society. The first sets out
a reasonable political conception of justice using the device of
the original position, but to say justification is *pro tanto* means
that it could be overridden by citizens' comprehensive doctrines
once all values are tallied up (Rawls 1996: 386). The second type
of justification involves the embedding of the political conception by the citizen into his comprehensive conception. The third
form of justification – public – is when all citizens embed the

political into their respective comprehensive conceptions. Only at this third stage will we know whether political liberalism is possible, for while many citizens may achieve an embedding of the political into their comprehensive conceptions, if there is insufficient collective embedding then the political system will be unstable. This is because of the free-rider problem (see pages 18–23), where free-riding is here motivated by moral principles rather than straightforward self-interest: if I know that enough other people hold comprehensive conceptions incompatible with respect for principles of justice, and so are likely to disobey the law, then I may be unwilling to forgo pressing *my* moral demands.

This is the key difference between Habermas and Rawls: for Habermas the possibility of political justification depends upon structures of reason which penetrate into a person's conception of the good, and as such the exercise of public reason does not wait until after citizens have *individually* embedded the political into their conceptions of the good. Habermas is right to argue this, but his conception of public reason is so strong that it erodes many reasonable (in an intuitive sense of the word) comprehensive conceptions. We are then faced with a choice: either we go with Rawls and argue that political justification is external to individuals' comprehensive conceptions of the good, with the danger that the overlapping consensus is historically fortuitous – a mere *modus vivendi* – or else we follow Habermas, but this threatens to erode many religious forms of life.

Dieter Henrich, a critic of Habermas, distinguishes two kinds of metaphysics: a metaphysics of conditions and a metaphysics of closure. The former is concerned with the necessary conditions for coming to valid judgement about what is true or untrue, right or wrong (Henrich 1999: 293). Such a metaphysics is essentially analytical: it breaks down knowledge into discrete claims. The latter form of metaphysics, in contrast, aims for a synthesis of diverse experiences (Henrich 1999: 294). Henrich believes both forms of metaphysics are essential: we cannot do without a meta-physics of conditions, but the results of such metaphysical enqui-ries are incomplete and generate conflicting 'primary descrip-tions' of human beings. For example, one primary description is citizenship – we are equal citizens and must act impartially – but we are also friends, family members, thinkers, sexual beings, employees or employers and so on. Each primary description generates specific rational and moral requirements, but these requirements may conflict. Human beings turn to a metaphysics of closure to integrate these conflicting primary descriptions.

Although Henrich does not state it in these terms, it is possible to interpret religious belief-systems as examples of a metaphysics of closure. Adopting this interpretation we can see that valid-ity-claims are examples of a metaphysics of conditions, whereas the lifeworld attempts a synthetic closure. Henrich criticizes Habermas for emphasizing validity-claims at the expense of world-views (or what Henrich calls 'moral images' of society). This is particularly evident when Habermas observes that the 'author-ity of the holy [has] gradually [been] replaced by the authority of an achieved consensus' (Habermas 1984: 77). This process he terms the 'linguistification of the sacred'. Arguably, only the most theologically liberal stream of Protestant Christianity would recognize this as a description of historical change and moral validity. Although Henrich's argument is directed at Habermas, his two-fold distinction also illuminates problems with Rawls's political liberalism.

First, Rawls runs together two kinds of metaphysical enquiry. The philosophical theories of, for example, Kant and Mill, and theological systems such as Calvinism or Sunni Islam, are all treated as 'comprehensive conceptions of the good'. If we accept Henrich's distinction then we need to distinguish systems that aim to uncover the underlying conditions of belief and action, and those that attempt to synthesize the apparently conflicting domains of human experience. The former may not be true but they are susceptible to criticism in the way the latter are not. This does not render theological systems invalid, but rather it is to maintain that they aim at something different to philosophical theories: synthesis rather than analysis. Engagement in arguments over the conditions of action is an unavoidable part of political theory, but it must be done in a way that recognizes the complex and possibly contradictory relationship between the two forms of metaphysical enquiry. Second, the oscillation between the burdens of judgement and the appeal to tradition can be explained. Suitably recast, the burdens can be reconstructed as a metaphysics of conditions. But the conditions threaten to erode the binding force of traditions, which have a different structure, namely, a synthetic one. Because the two are in conflict, the relationship between the burdens of judgement and the description of a reasonable comprehensive conception of the good is unstable.

In closing it is worth saying something about Rawls's own religious beliefs. Rawls went through a distinct phase as an undergraduate in which he was (in his own words) 'deeply concerned about theology and its doctrines' (Rawls, 2009: 261). As suggested in Chapter 1 he abandoned any orthodox Christian beliefs during his military service in the latter part of the Second World War. In his undergraduate thesis ('A Brief Inquiry into the Meaning of Sin and Faith') he posits the fundamental presupposition that 'there is a being whom Christians call God and who has revealed Himself in Christ Jesus' (Rawls, 2009: 111). And he distinguishes a natural view of the world and an interpersonal one. Humans can interact with the world naturally by desiring certain things or having an aversion to things, but they also enter relationships of reciprocity or mutual regard (I-thou relationships):

> The relation between the 'I' and the 'thou' is therefore personal, that between the 'I' as desiring and the thing desired such as

food and drink is natural, while the relation between any two
things is causal, such as the relation between food and drink and
the table upon which it rests (Rawls, 2009: 114).

This is very close to the intersubjectivity that underpins
Habermas's discourse ethics. This is not entirely surprising as
both are influenced by a pre-War theology that focuses on the
intersubjective I-thou relationship. But, importantly, in his later
work Rawls rejects these arguments as the basis of political liberalism, although they might form part of an overlapping consensus of reasonable doctrines. In his piece 'On my Religion' (written in 1997), Rawls says 'my religion is of interest only to me'
(Rawls 2009: 261).

Further reading

For a basic discussion of political liberalism written prior to the
publication of *Political Liberalism*, see Kukathas and Pettit (1990),
Chapter 7. For a more involved discussion of Rawls's later work,
see Dreben in Freeman (2003), and also Larmore (on public
reason) in Freeman (2003). There is a collection of essays on
political liberalism, Davion and Wolff (2000), and a book-length
treatment of Rawls on religion: Dombrowski (2001). Further
essays can be found on various aspects of Rawls's later philosophical concerns: on stability, see articles by Freeman, McLennan,
Hill and Scheffler in Richardson and Weithman (1999; vol. 4).
On politics and metaphysics see Raz, Hampton, Rorty and
Weithman in Richardson and Weithman (1999; vol. 5). And for
a discussion of the relationship between Rawls and Habermas see
Young, McCarthy and Habermas in Richardson and Weithman
(1999; vol. 5) (the last of those essays is Habermas's engagement
with Rawls, to which the last 'Lecture' in *Political Liberalism* is a
response). See also Kukathas (2003; vol. 4), parts 1, 2, 3 (pluralism), 4 (religion), 7 and 8.

9

The law of peoples

Most of Rawls's work focuses on domestic justice – that is, justice between individuals in a 'closed society'. In his last substantively new work – *The Law of Peoples* (1999) – he turns his attention to international relations. In *A Theory of Justice* Rawls had touched on international law with a very brief discussion of what he there called the 'law of nations' (Rawls 1972: 378), arguing for the extension of the idea of the original position to international relations, but with the parties in the original position being nations rather than individual human beings. However, it was clear from the tone of his remarks that working out the derivation of international law was a project for the future, and the main reason Rawls felt compelled to introduce it in the earlier work was to explain the limits of obligation to the state: what justifies refusal to serve in the armed forces in a liberal society? Interestingly, that remains the concern of *The Law of Peoples*: we need an elaboration of international law in order to establish whether liberal societies ought to tolerate non-liberal ones. It is important to recognize the relatively limited ambitions of the book. Many readers may expect a deeper discussion of the issue of cultural relativism, that is, to what extent the justification of the two principles of justice is limited to a particular kind of society. Certainly, *The Law of Peoples* casts light on that issue, but then a reading of his other works, and especially *Political Liberalism*, provides a fuller, although not necessarily more coherent, reflection on the problem of cultural relativism. Rawls's derivation of international law has to be seen in the context of his main body of work, and in this chapter I will emphasize the continuities and discontinuities between the law of peoples and his theory of domestic justice.

Liberal peoples

In *A Theory of Justice* Rawls talks of the law of *nations*, whereas he now employs the term '*peoples*'. The term 'people' is used in contrast to 'state': a people has a moral character, whereas a state, Rawls suggests, is narrowly rational. Duties are owed fundamentally to peoples and only derivatively to states. This is a questionable distinction, since states certainly can be held morally responsible, and indeed under international law are artificial persons, where the concept of 'person' implies responsibility before others. Interestingly, one compelling reason for employing the concept of a people rather than a state is to allow for stateless peoples to make moral claims within the international community: the Kurds are, for example, a people without a state. Rawls implies that peoples can secede and thus peoples rather than states make up the international community (Rawls 1999a: 38), but he does not make the conceptual connection of this issue with the state/people distinction. The main reason he insists on peoples rather than states is to distance himself from the realist international law tradition that has been dominant since the formation of the world system of nation-states after the Treaty of Westphalia (1648). That tradition emphasizes the right of a state to wage war to protect or advance its interests even if it has not been directly attacked, and to determine its internal domestic arrangements even if that entails the violation of the rights of its citizens. The concept of a *people* emphasizes that citizens have moral claims against their own state.

Rawls extends the device of the original position to generate the law of peoples. At first sight, it may be thought that
he simply treats all peoples, whether liberal or non-liberal, as
agents in an international original position. As with agents in
the domestic original position the peoples have primary goods
of which they seek to maximize their shares and they are free to
choose any principles to govern their relations. In fact, the derivation of the law of peoples is more complicated: there are two
choice situations – the first is between liberal peoples and the
second between non-liberal, but decent, peoples. Furthermore,
in contrast to the domestic original position there is a single set
of principles that the peoples are asked to endorse rather than
a menu from which they can choose. I will discuss how non-
liberal (but decent) peoples come to endorse a set of rules for
international conduct, but the focus in this section is entirely on
liberal societies. It may make it easier to think of these societies
as forming a distinct international community and the rules are
those that they apply to *their* relations.

First, we need principles of domestic justice, and these I have
discussed extensively. Viewed from a purely domestic perspective
there is no need for armed forces. Certainly, we know that principles of justice will be coercively enforced and so a police force and
judiciary are required, but armed forces are necessary only to repel
external threats. In a just society the army is not used against its
own people (Rawls 1999a: 26). However, Rawls assumes we live
in a world of states (or peoples) and consequently there must be
an international dimension to *domestic* policy, and as I suggested at
the beginning of the chapter, Rawls's reason for discussing international justice is to explain what constitutes an ethical foreign
policy for a just society. But there is a further reason for discussing
international relations and it connects to the idea of a just society:
the content of the law of peoples (outlined below) restricts the
power of a state over its own citizens, such that by endorsing the
law a state agrees to limit its own powers, in much the same way as

individuals in the domestic original position agree to pursue their interests within the constraints of the principles of justice.

The international original position – what Rawls calls the second original position – shares many features of the domestic, or first, original position. The parties in the original position are representatives of real peoples but through the use of the veil of ignorance are denied knowledge of which people they represent. Like agents in the original position, representatives in the second original position are motivated to advance the interests of whichever people they represent. Thus the fundamentals of the two original positions are the same but they differ in their detailed application to their respective subjects – that is, domestic and international law. It may be argued that Rawls's argument is anthropomorphic: the 'people' is treated as if it were a human being. This is especially striking when Rawls says:

> [Individual human beings] see themselves as self-authenticating sources of claims, and capable of taking responsibility for their ends. In the Law of Peoples we do somewhat the same: we view peoples as conceiving themselves as free and equal peoples in the Society of Peoples (Rawls 1999a: 33–4).

The credibility of the parallel between an individual human agent and a people depends strongly on Rawls's conception of reasonableness as used in *Political Liberalism*, and the rejection of 'metaphysical' conceptions of the reasonable and the rational. Rawls argues there is no generic concept of reasonableness, permitting an axiomatic derivation of principles of justice (Rawls 1999a: 30). Siding implicitly with the later work of Ludwig Wittgenstein he maintains we know what is reasonable by the context. This suggests there are parallels, or affinities, between domestic and international justice that allow us to talk of peoples as agents without asserting the metaphysical existence of collective entities. We need not be metaphysical holists – that is, believe that collective entities are not reducible to individual human beings. Likewise with rationality, all we require is that preferences can be ordered and pursued, and we know from international relations that it makes sense to talk of the interests of collective entities. Rawls's parallelism does however raise difficulties, especially when we turn to his idea of a decent hierarchical people, but for the moment let us accept the idea of an international contract between *liberal* peoples makes sense and consider what principles they would endorse. Rawls sets out eight principles that should hold between free and democratic peoples (Rawls 1999a: 37):

1. Peoples are free and independent, and their freedom and independence are to be respected by other peoples.
2. Peoples are to observe treaties and undertakings.
3. Peoples are equal and are parties to the agreements that bind them.
4. Peoples are to observe a duty of non-intervention.
5. Peoples have the right to self-defence but no right to instigate war for reasons other than self-defence.
6. Peoples are to honour human rights.
7. Peoples are to observe certain specified restrictions in the conduct of war.
8. Peoples have a duty to assist other peoples living under unfavourable conditions that prevent their having a just or decent political and social regime.

As suggested earlier the principles are not selected from a menu of possible principles but the parties are asked to endorse *and interpret* the eight principles. It is not entirely clear why the parties in the second original position are not free to choose alternative principles, but it may be that Rawls intends the domestic and global original positions to be disanalogous: the choice in the former expresses human autonomy, even if, as he suggests in *Political Liberalism*, that autonomy is understood in a weak, political sense. Peoples, on the other hand, are independent and equal, but not autonomous.

How the representatives in the global original position interpret the principles will be limited by domestic justice – that is, the two principles that have been selected in the first (domestic) original position. And there are some important differences between the two original positions. First, a liberal people has no comprehensive conception of the good, whereas individuals do have such conceptions, albeit they are denied knowledge of them. Second, a liberal people's fundamental interests are specified by its political conception of justice whereas individuals' interests are determined by their conceptions of the good. The basic point is that *for liberal societies* the international original position is parasitic upon the domestic original position: what a liberal people seeks to protect in the international sphere are the just political institutions created by individuals in the domestic original position. The domestic principles of justice constrain the interpretation of the eight principles of international law: for example, a people committed to the two principles of (domestic) justice would not endorse a utilitarian interpretation of any of the eight principles of international justice because no people would accept that the benefit gained by one people *in itself* – as a first principle – justifies a cost to another people (Rawls 1999a: 40). However, interestingly, Rawls does not extend the strong egalitarianism of the difference principle to the international sphere.

There is a tight connection between domestic and international justice where liberal societies are concerned, and Rawls appeals to empirical studies to support this contention. A body of thought going back to late seventeenth- and eighteenth-century thinkers such as Montesquieu, Kant and Adam Smith stresses the stabilizing effects of commerce: peoples engaged in trade develop habits and acquire interests conducive to peaceful relations with fellow trading powers. Furthermore, when trading nations develop liberal-democratic institutions – there is a link between capitalism and liberalism – domestic forces conducive to a defensive rather than an aggressive foreign policy are strengthened. Rawls cites the work of Michael Doyle, whose study of international conflicts since 1800 supports what is termed the 'democratic peace argument' (Rawls 1999a: 51–4). Surveying the data Doyle could not find a single conflict in which two liberal democratic societies went to war against one another. His thesis has been criticized – much depends on which states are categorized as liberal democratic and the thesis does not allow for covert or proxy wars between states – but even if examples of inter-democratic wars could be found the great weight of evidence supports the contention that there is *something* about liberal democracy supportive of peace. The task for Rawls is to articulate in theoretical terms this empirical evidence, and I think he argues convincingly that democratically accountable governments will find peaceful ways to resolve their disputes. The real difficulty for Rawls's theory of international justice begins when he attempts to extend it to non-liberal peoples, although, of course, the central objective of *The Law of Peoples* is to argue the possibility that such peoples can be members of a society of peoples.

Non-liberal peoples

Rawls does not claim that the eight principles of international law will be endorsed by all peoples. His ambitions are more limited. He wants to demonstrate that a non-liberal society can endorse those principles and, therefore, a liberal society can tolerate a non-liberal one. The reference to toleration is important:

> To tolerate means not only to refrain from exercising political sanctions – military, economic, or diplomatic – to make a people change its ways. To tolerate also means to recognize

these non-liberal societies as equal participating members in good standing of the Society of Peoples, with certain rights and obligations, including the duty of civility requiring that they offer other peoples public reasons appropriate to the Society of Peoples for their actions (Rawls 1999a: 59).

Many liberal political theorists would reject this second idea of toleration – certainly the stability of the international order may require refraining from what is commonly referred to as 'regime change', but we have no reason to tolerate non-liberal societies at that deeper level of 'civility'. Since a non-liberal people does not treat its citizens as free and equal then it cannot *itself* be treated as an equal among the community of peoples. This is the core objection to Rawls's extension of international law to non-liberal societies and I will return to it at several points in the discussion. The aim at this stage is to outline Rawls's conception of a decent non-liberal society.

Rawls places non-liberal peoples in four categories: (a) decent peoples (or societies); (b) outlaw states; (c) burdened societies; (d) benevolent absolutisms (Rawls 1999a: 4). Although the category breaks down into several variants Rawls takes as his model of a decent society one particular variant which he calls a 'decent hierarchical society'. Of the non-liberal societies only decent peoples are capable of endorsing the eight principles of international law. Outlaw states, of which North Korea would be a compelling contemporary example, routinely threaten other states and violate the human rights of their own citizens. Of course, since the eight principles rule out such behaviour, outlaw states, by definition, cannot endorse the principles. But liberal societies cannot ignore such states, for they put strain on the international order. Furthermore, the *peoples* of those states cannot be held responsible for the actions of their governments. Should it be necessary to go to war against an outlaw state rules of engagement must constrain what can be done to the peoples of those states (Rawls 1999a: 95). Burdened societies – or 'societies burdened by unfavourable conditions' (Rawls 1999a: 106) – raise different ethical issues to those posed by outlaw states. Although Rawls argues that a decent society does not require a very high level of resources, and starvation is more often the result of cultural or political factors than an absolute absence of food (Rawls 1999a: 9), we still need to ensure societies have the institutional conditions whereby they can become decent peoples. Finally, benevolent absolutisms show a significant degree of respect for human rights and do not engage in aggression against other states. However, they lack any mechanisms for consultation and are not well-ordered, with the consequence that they cannot be trusted to respect the eight principles.

To illustrate a decent people – more specifically, a decent hierarchical people – Rawls presents the reader with an imaginary Muslim society: Kazanistan. This society is associationist, meaning its members are viewed in public life as belonging to different groups, each of which is represented in the legal system by a body in a decent consultation hierarchy (Rawls 1999a: 64). There are two criteria for a decent hierarchical society to be a member in good standing in a reasonable society of peoples: (a) the society does not have aggressive aims; (b) human rights are respected, and there is a system of law which imposes duties and obligations (distinct from human rights) on all persons (Rawls 1999a: 64–7). In a liberal society human rights are derived from the domestic original position, and are thus dependent on a particular conception of the human agent as autonomous. In a decent hierarchical society human rights are not justified by appeal to a particular conception of the human agent – there is no domestic original position – but rather they are regarded as necessary to any effective system of social co-operation.

The second criterion requires, alongside respect for human rights, representative institutions. Although these are not democratic they do possess formal mechanisms of consultation and regard individuals as rational and 'capable of moral learning as recognized in their society' (Rawls 1999a: 71). And it is through individuals' associations that their interests are respected. Rawls's imaginary society of Kazanistan is characterized by such a consultation hierarchy. Its system of law recognizes no distinction between 'church' and 'state' (using Rawls's Western terms): Islam is the favoured religion and the higher offices are held by Muslims. However, other religions are tolerated in as much as their adherents are free to worship and are encouraged to take part in civic life. Kazanistan satisfies the six guidelines required to be a decent people and thus a member of the society of peoples: (a) all groups are consulted; (b) each member of society must belong to a group; (c) each group must be represented by a body that contains at least some of the group's own members; (d) the body making the final decisions – the rulers – must weigh the views of each group; (e) the decisions should be based on a conception of the special priorities of Kazanistan, which include the need to establish a 'decent and rational' Muslim society that respects religious minorities; (f) the special priorities should fit into a general scheme of co-operation which is explicitly specified (Rawls 1999a: 77).

Rawls presents Kazanistan as an imaginary people, but it is instructive to consider whether any real societies come close to it. Many of the the Arabian Gulf states come close, but other states are far harder to classify. Saudi Arabia has a consultation hierarchy, but also engages in quite serious violations of human rights. Not only are punishments such as amputation of hands and public beheadings extreme, but the legal process is far from equitable or transparent. Yet Saudi Arabia is neither an outlaw state, nor a burdened society (although it is a major source of Wahabi-inspired non-state terrorism). In fairness to Rawls, it may be argued that his typology is intended to be illustrative rather than exhaustive and the law of peoples is not equivalent to existing international law. However, the case of Saudi Arabia draws attention not merely to an empirical issue of typology, but a philosophical problem: does the validity of the law of peoples derive from its contribution to world order – that is, respect for the sovereignty of other states – or from respect for individual rights? If the former is the case, then Saudi Arabia should be regarded as a member of the society of peoples, but if the latter, then clearly it cannot be a member, for there is widespread violation of human rights.

I will return to this philosophical difficulty later, but for now we will accept that only a decent (liberal or hierarchical) society can be a member of the society of peoples, meaning that such a society can endorse the eight principles of the law of peoples. To explain the process whereby it comes to endorse the law Rawls once again uses the device of the original position. However, liberal and decent peoples cannot together endorse the eight principles. This is because the veil of ignorance *for liberal societies* precludes knowledge of conceptions of the good – for example, the predominant religion of a society – whereas we could not stipulate that decent societies be denied this knowledge. So there are three original positions: two for liberal societies (domestic and international) and one for decent societies (international) (Rawls 1999a: 70). The veil functions to deny decent societies knowledge of their material resources and geographical (therefore, strategic) position.

Just war

In these two final sections I turn to issues of policy: when is a war just? And are wealthy states obliged to redistribute resources to poorer states? Whereas the discussion until now has taken place within ideal theory – that is, the presumption of compliance with the law of peoples – how we conduct wars and what obligations exist to transfer wealth to poorer societies fall under non-ideal theory. It is not difficult to see why discussion of just war is part of non-ideal theory – war is only necessary where there exist outlaw states – but it is harder to grasp why resource transfers should be part of non-ideal theory. After all, the second principle of justice for liberal societies involves significant transfers of wealth, and that discussion is part of ideal theory. As we will see Rawls regards international resource transfers as a means by which societies achieve the minimum material conditions for participation in the international community. It follows that transfers are only necessary if a society is 'burdened' and burdened societies do not exist under ideal theory. Rawls presents a highly egalitarian theory of justice for liberal societies but a relatively inegalitarian theory of international justice. We begin with a discussion of the aims and conduct of war.

Peoples, Rawls argues, have a right to go to war in self-defence but not, as in traditional accounts of state sovereignty, simply in the rational pursuit of a state's interests (Rawls 1999a: 90). And in a liberal society conscription into the armed forces is only justified when just institutions are under attack – the need to defend liberty justifies a short-term, but transparent and proportional, interference in an individual's liberty. Since decent hierarchical societies do not share the same conception of domestic justice they may make further demands on their citizens. However, since both decent and liberal societies fight only defensive wars they will have no reason to amass armed forces beyond what is necessary to deter aggression. Civic republicans may object to Rawls's narrow understanding of the function of armed forces in a liberal society, and argue that a period of military service not only educates citizens in democratic duties but counteracts the danger that a professional army may become detached from society. Presumably Rawls would isolate the offensive functions from other functions of the armed forces, and his concern is directed specifically at the former.

A war is just if the reasons for waging it are just by reference to the law of peoples, and – importantly – if it is conducted in conformity with certain rules of combat. Well-ordered (decent and liberal) peoples must carefully distinguish three groups: an outlaw state's leaders and officials, its soldiers, and its civilian population. Since the population is not a 'people' in Rawls's sense – it is not consulted in matters of public policy – it cannot be held responsible for the instigation of an aggressive war. For this reason Rawls argues that the fire-bombing of Tokyo and other Japanese cities in the spring of 1945 and the atomic bombing of Hiroshima and Nagasaki were 'very grave wrongs' (Rawls 1999a: 95). Enemy combatants must also be treated with respect because, firstly, they have human rights and, secondly, the possibility of long-term peace – which is one of the aims of a just war – is assisted if the armed forces of an outlaw state are treated with a respect which they themselves may not accord to forces of the well-ordered society.

Practical means-end reasoning must always be limited by these ethical considerations. Rawls stresses the importance of statesmanship in international relations, and although he does not make the connection in this book, drawing on his earlier work we can say that in a well-ordered society those who hold public office in just institutions have special obligations, and recognition of these obligations is part of citizenship. There is an assumption in Rawls's work that decent societies are sufficiently well-ordered for statesmanship to be practiced. Statesmen have the ability to look beyond the next election and recognize that 'once peace is securely re-established, the enemy society is to be granted an autonomous well-ordered regime of its own' (Rawls 1999a: 98).

There are circumstances of war in which a society is permitted to set aside the strict status of citizens that normally prevents their being attacked. This set of circumstances Rawls terms the 'supreme emergency exemption'. In 1940–41, when Britain was alone and had few means of breaking German military power the bombing of German cities was 'arguably' justified (Rawls

1999a: 98). It was necessary for domestic morale and as a sign that Britain was willing to fight Germany 'until the end' (Rawls 1999a: 99). It might be possible, Rawls suggests, to justify the bombing of German cities until the German defeat at Battle of Stalingrad in February 1943, but the attack on Dresden in February 1945 certainly fell outside the period of 'supreme emergency'. The nature of the National Socialist regime justified the exemption on the part of the *British* within a *particular time period*, but this exemption never held for the Americans in relation to Japan and it was the weight of means-ends reasoning that led to the atomic bombing of the two Japanese cities (Rawls 1999a: 100). To argue that the bombings saved thousands of American servicemen's lives is to hold a Japanese life to be of less value than an American life. Furthermore, to apply hindsight and say that in the context of the times because of atrocities committed by the Japanese it was understandable for the Allies to show little respect for the enemy is to allow passions to override statesmanship. The bombings were authorised by President Harry Truman, and it was his task, as a statesman, to prevent popular feeling determining the conduct of war.

One final point on the conduct of war connects up with the discussion of civil disobedience in a nearly just – that is, liberal – society (see Chapter 7). Some people in a liberal society are pacifists, or have objections to the conduct of war that go further than those set out above. The Catholic doctrine of double-effect forbids civilian casualties except insofar as they are the unintended and indirect result of a legitimate attack on a military target. The supreme emergency exemption violates this doctrine (Rawls 1999a: 104–5). Quakers oppose all war and refuse military service. While there may be good, practical grounds for exempting conscientious objectors from military service, if you take the commitment to the principles of justice seriously you must be prepared to fight to defend them. Rawls provides no adequate response to these challenges to his theory of (domestic) justice, except to say that pacifists cannot 'in good faith' accept public office. The problem is that denial of public office is a violation of the second principle of justice: fair equality of opportunity.

Global distributive justice and migration

What obligations are owed by wealthy states to poor states? Relatively well-ordered societies have a duty to bring burdened societies, along with outlaw societies, into the society of peoples (Rawls 1999a: 106). It does not follow that they must transfer resources to burdened societies in order to achieve this goal. Part of the reasoning is that transfers are indeterminate – we do not know at what point transfers must cease. This seems an odd point – surely, so long as we know our transfers are having some effect we should make them? A second, and more substantial, argument against transfers is that a society with few resources can be well-ordered if 'its political traditions, law, and property and class structure with their underlying religious and moral beliefs and culture are such as to sustain a liberal or decent society' (Rawls 1999a: 106). Rawls goes on to make a subtly different point: the culture of a society is a very significant determinant of the wealth of that society. These are indeed distinct points. The first establishes the limits of a well-ordered society's duties to a burdened society – transfers are aimed at creating a well-ordered society and not directly at benefiting the individual members of that society. The second is an observation – possibly correct – of the causes of poverty. On this second point Rawls makes various elaborations: a society's population policy is extremely important; failure in food distribution rather than food decline is the cause of most famines; and the unemployed in *prosperous societies* would starve without domestic income transfers (Rawls 1999a: 9, 109–10).

Rawls rejects the extension of the difference principle to international relations, arguing that the target of distribution is the achievement of a society's political autonomy and consequent upon that is its joining the society of peoples. This argument fits with his rejection of the extension of domestic liberal justice to the international sphere: peoples are represented in the society of peoples, not individual human beings. A practical result of Rawls's position is that while he has an egalitarian theory of domestic justice he has an inegalitarian theory of international justice. One might admire Rawls's hard-headedness: it is difficult to motivate citizens in prosperous societies to accept income transfers to poor societies, and that reluctance is not based solely on a lack of confidence in recipient governments to ensure the money benefits the worst-off in those burdened societies.

There have been plenty of 'Rawlsian' critics of Rawls. Some of these critiques predate the publication of *The Law of Peoples* and are directed at *A Theory of Justice*, but the points made are germane to Rawls's later work. Charles Beitz is strongly influenced by Rawls but criticizes his refusal to extend his theory of domestic justice to the international sphere. Beitz accepts that Rawls's position on global redistribution has its roots in his assumptions about the circumstances of justice, meaning the circumstances under which it makes sense to talk about justice and injustice. A central point for Rawls is the idea that justice is about the fair distribution of the benefits and burdens of social co-operation (Beitz, 1999: 131). This description, Beitz argues, introduces elements of a social ideal into what should be a mere description of a social condition. Slaves in ancient Greece were part of society but neither willingly co-operated nor (arguably) benefited from the polis: 'it would be better to say that the requirements of justice apply to institutions and practices (whether or not they are genuinely co-operative) in which social activity produces relative or absolute benefits or burdens that would not exist if the social activity did not take place' (Beitz,

1999: 131). The international economy is not a co-operative scheme in Rawls's narrow sense but it is one in Beitz's wide sense of 'co-operation'. This has radical implications: Rawls's two principles of justice cannot be restricted to the nation-state but must – in some form – be implemented globally.

Distinct from the issue of global redistribution but raising similar issues is the question of migration, particularly from less developed to more developed countries. Arguably it was the changes in immigration law in the 1960s, such as the 1965 Immigration and Nationality Act that ended the national quotas of the 1924 Immigration Act, that have had a greater impact on American politics and society than the more famous Civil Rights Movement. And indeed some of the challenges raised in Chapter 8 regarding the stability of political principles have been rendered more acute by the increasing cultural and religious diversity that immigration has brought about. In all of Rawls's works the reader is hard-pressed to find a discussion of immigration and yet implicit in his argument is a restrictivist policy. The few explicit remarks he makes can be found in *The Law of Peoples*. Given the sensitivity of debates about immigration in the United States, Europe and other European-derived societies it is interesting to reflect on Rawls's arguments.

Just as Beitz criticised Rawls as insufficiently Rawlsian on global justice, so Joseph Carens argues that he does not follow through the logic of his own argument in relation to immigration. Carens maintains that if the original position precludes choosing principles on the basis of contingent facts such as a person's sex or race or social class, then it follows that membership of a particular society should also be treated as a morally irrelevant fact: 'we should take a global, not a national, view of the original position' (Carens, 1995: 335). Carens grants there is a 'general case for decentralization of power' which would justify the existence of 'autonomous political communities comparable to modern states' (Carens, 1995: 335). The question is whether such communities would have the right to limit entry and exit. If free movement within a state is justified then it follows that unhindered movement between states must be legitimate. Carens' core argument is based on the moral equality of human beings, and how, given that equality, agents in the original position would necessarily universalise that right. More concretely, he argues that the perspective of the worst-off and the priority given to liberty would rule out restrictions on immigration, except in the case that liberty or order were seriously threatened. The argument is simple but powerful, resting as it does on equality and universalisation and it demands a convincing response.

While Rawls does not respond directly Carens we can reconstruct an answer from his earlier work and his brief remarks in *The Law of Peoples*. While the original position appears to be an expression of radical individualism – and thus universal equality – it has be seen against a background set of assumptions, some of which are relevant to the question of immigration. Society is a scheme of social co-operation; such co-operation imposes duties on both the most and the least advantaged, and 'this assumption [of co-operation] implies that all are willing to work and to do their part in sharing the burdens of social life, provided of course the terms of co-operation are seen as fair' (Rawls, 2001: 179). Co-operation implies that the goods to be distributed are the product of labour. If an individual capable of work refuses a reasonable offer of work and instead spends all day surfing off Malibu then he has made the choice to trade income for leisure and cannot expect financial support through income transfers from those who do work. The relevance of social co-operation to immigration is indirect. The point is not that immigrants live off welfare, but that conceiving of society as co-operative in the sense that it depends on material reproduction through labour complicates the calculations that agents in the original position make. Some immigrants may strengthen the terms of co-operation if their lifetime benefits outweigh their costs. This will happen if they bring skills that raise the national product without worsening the position of the least advantaged. Other immigrants may carry costs. It is important that we can predict with whom we are engaged in deliberation. While determinacy does not require knowing the identities of other agents in the original position, nor our particular society, it does presuppose not only that I (whoever I am) live my entire life within this society (whatever society that may be), but that I am interacting with the same people, who are similarly situated. The possibility of migration undermines that determinacy and so weakens social cooperation.

As I have argued and as indicated by its title central to *The Law of Peoples* is the concept of a 'people'. Rawls argues that 'an important role of government, however arbitrary a society's boundaries may appear from a historical point of view, is to be the effective agent of the people as they take responsibility for their territory and the size of their population, as well as maintaining the land's environmental integrity'. Unless a defined agent is made responsible for maintaining an asset it will tend to deteriorate, and the asset 'is the people's territory and its potential capacity to support them *in perpetuity*; and the agent is the people itself as politically organized' (Rawls, 1999: 8; his emphasis). The 'in perpetuity' condition is of importance to the legitimacy of immigration control. The law of peoples precludes dealing with the problem of population growth through conquest in war or 'by migrating into another people's territory without their consent' (Rawls, 1999: 8). Rawls makes clear that a people are morally entitled to limit immigration and adds that it can also be limited to protect a people's culture and its constitutional principles (Rawls, 1999: 39n).

In effect, the problem of immigration falls under non-ideal theory. Immigration is caused by unjust and unfavourable conditions. The persecution of religious and ethnic minorities understandably causes people to seek sanctuary. Starvation – as in the

Irish famine of the 1840s – also triggers the mass movement of people. But following the arguments of Amartya Sen (Sen, 1999: 180–1), Rawls argues that famine is not caused by an absolute shortage of food, but by political failure to provide a safety net when a loss of income results in the inability to buy food. Population pressures often have their roots in gender inequality; as men and women become more equal so the birth rate falls. And Rawls concludes: 'religious freedom and liberty of conscience, political freedom and constitutional liberties, and equal justice for women are fundamental aspects of sound social policy for a realistic utopia. The problem of immigration is not, then, simply left aside, but is eliminated as a serious problem in a realistic utopia' (Rawls, 1999: 9).

Further reading

The only book-length work on Rawls's law of peoples is Hayden (2002). Part 1 of Hayden outlines Rawls's domestic theory, so part 2 is the most useful. In Richardson and Weithman (1999; vol. 3) see articles by Beitz and Pogge. In Kukathas (2003; vol. 4), read parts 5 and 6.

Postscript

Will Rawls be widely discussed one hundred years from now, or will his arguments appear anachronistic? Assuming the cultural conditions still exist for the discussion of philosophy, such a speculative question can be useful in determining what – if anything – is enduring in Rawls's work. It may be that political philosophy is more vulnerable to historical change than, say, the philosophy of mind, but the case of Hobbes shows that works of political philosophy can endure, just as changes in our conception of the mind-body relationship can render a theory of mind redundant. In assessing Rawls's long-term significance we must distinguish the deep structure of his thought from the 'parochial', where the latter is particularly susceptible to the vagaries of history.

While there is something aesthetically appealing about the difference principle in that it is a determinate principle of justice – unlike the idea of a social minimum – I would suggest that it is only applicable to a society at a particular level of development. The equal liberty principle has deeper roots, but is not strikingly original. In short, Rawls's principles of justice may have less staying power than his method for deriving them. At the heart of Rawls's method is a conception of the human agent as autonomous, yet whose autonomy must be realized and exercised in society. The original position is a device for expressing and at the same time limiting the 'social'. The basic structure of society, while inherited, can also be seen as the product of human will, and crucially the agent can be *motivated* to respect the principles underlying that society. Motivation is the key theme of Rawls's work. Insofar as this is Rawls's project, he is offering a renewed Kantianism.

In his later work Rawls's concern with motivation remains, but he abandons the Kantian response. In its place he offers a more pluralistic methodology. *Political Liberalism* fits with a contemporary concern with religious difference and while such difference is nothing new an added urgency has been given by the effects of global migration, which has made Western societies more socially, ethnically and culturally diverse. What is more, the challenge posed to liberal democracies by fundamentalist-inspired terrorism lends the later work topicality. Without downplaying terrorism – which is both a direct threat, but also an indirect one, insofar as it provokes a restriction on civil liberties – viewed from a longer perspective it may be a less significant challenge to Rawlsian liberalism than the ecological crisis. Although a just society need not be an economically expanding one, the combined challenges of population growth and a continuing degradation of natural resources may render it impossible to guarantee even the minimal conditions for a just society. The philosophical challenge is this: can a liberal Kantian theory of moral motivation provide sufficient incentives to ensure the environmental conditions for a liberal society? Readers of Rawls one hundred years from now may conclude that his project was a manifestation of a golden age of material prosperity.

Bibliography

Works by Rawls

Rawls, John (1972). *A Theory of Justice*, Oxford: Oxford University Press

Rawls, John (1996). *Political Liberalism*, Paperback Edition, New York: Columbia University Press

Rawls, John (1999a). *The Law of Peoples*, Cambridge Mass. & London: Harvard University Press

Rawls, John (1999b). *Collected Papers*, edited by Samuel Freeman, Cambridge Mass. & London: Harvard University Press

Rawls, John (1999c). *A Theory of Justice*, Revised Edition, Oxford: Oxford University Press

Rawls , John (2000). *Lectures on the History of Moral Philosophy*, edited by Barbara Herman, Cambridge Mass. & London: Harvard University Press

Rawls, John (2001). *Justice as Fairness: a Restatement*, edited by Erin Kelly, Cambridge Mass. & London: Belknap Press of Harvard University Press

Rawls, John (2009). *A Brief Inquiry into the Meaning of Sin and Faith*, edited by Thomas Nagel, Cambridge Mass. & London: Harvard University Press

Secondary works cited in the text and in the further readings

Barry, Brian (1973). *The Liberal Theory of Justice: a Critical Examination of the Principal Doctrines in 'A Theory of Justice'*, Oxford: Clarendon Press

Barry, Brian (1989). *A Treatise on Social Justice: Vol. 1: Theories of Justice*, London: Harvester Wheatsheaf

Barry, Brian (1990). 'How Not to Defend Liberal Institutions', *British Journal of Political Science*, 20, 1–14

Beitz, Charles (1999). *Political Theory and International Relations*, Princeton, NJ: Princeton University Press

Carens, Joseph (1995). 'Aliens and Citizens: The Case for Open Borders', in Will Kymlicka (editor), *The Rights of Minority Cultures*, Oxford: Oxford University Press, 1995

Carter, Ian (1995). 'The Independent Value of Freedom', *Ethics*, 105, 4, 819–45

Cohen, G. A. (2000). *If You're an Egalitarian, How Come You're so Rich?*, Cambridge Mass. & London: Harvard University Press

Daniels, Norman (1989). *Reading Rawls: Critical Studies on Rawls' 'A Theory of Justice'*, Stanford: Stanford University Press

Davion, Victoria and Wolf, Clark (2000): *The Idea of a Political Liberalism: Essays on Rawls*, Lenham & Oxford: Rowman and Littlefield

De Vries, Robert (2014), 'Earning by Degrees: Differences in the Career Outcomes of UK Graduates', The Sutton Trust

Dombrowski, Daniel (2001). *Rawls and Religion: the Case for Political Liberalism*, Albany: SUNY Press

Dworkin, Ronald et al (1997). 'Assisted Suicide: The Philosophers' Brief', *The New York Review of Books*, 44, 5, March 27 1997

Dworkin, Ronald (2000). *Sovereign Virtue: the Theory and Practice of Equality*, Cambridge Mass. & London: Harvard University Press

Flanagan, Owen and Jackson, Kathryn (1987). 'Justice, Care, and Gender: The Kohlberg–Gilligan Debate Revisited', *Ethics*, 97, 3, 622–37

Freeman, Samuel (2003). *The Cambridge Companion to Rawls*, Cambridge: Cambridge University Press

Gilligan, Carol (1982). *In a Different Voice: Psychological Theory and Women's Development*, Cambridge Mass. & London: Harvard University Press

Habermas, Jürgen (1984). *The Theory of Communicative Action, Volume 1: Reason and the Rationalization of Society*, London: Heinemann

Habermas, Jürgen (1994). 'Struggles for Recognition in the Democratic Constitutional State', in Amy Gutmann (editor), *Multiculturalism:*

Examining the Politics of Recognition, Princeton: Princeton University Press

Habermas, Jürgen (1995). 'Reconciliation Through the Public Use of Reason: Remarks on John Rawls's Political Liberalism', *The Journal of Philosophy*, 92, 3, 109–31

Haksar, Vinit (1986). *Civil Disobedience, Threats and Offers: Gandhi and Rawls*, Delhi & Oxford: Oxford University Press

Hayden, Patrick (2002). *John Rawls: Towards a Just World Order*, Cardiff: University of Wales Press

Henrich, Dieter (1999). 'What is Metaphysics – What is Modernity? Twelve Theses Against Jürgen Habermas', in Peter Dews (ed.), *Habermas: a Critical Reader*, Oxford: Blackwell

Hudson, W. D. (1967). *Ethical Intuitionism*, London: Macmillan

Kant, Immanuel (1996). *Practical Philosophy*, translated and edited by Mary Gregor, Cambridge: Cambridge University Press

King, Martin Luther (1991). 'Letter from Birmingham City Jail', in H. A. Bedau (editor), *Civil Disobedience in Focus*, London: Routledge

Kukathas, Chandran and Pettit, Phillip (1990). *Rawls: a Theory of Justice and its Critics*, Cambridge: Polity Press

Kukathas, Chandran (2003). *John Rawls: Critical Assessments of Leading Political Philosophers*, London & New York: Routledge, Volumes 1–4

Locke, John (1992). *Two Treatises of Government*, edited by Peter Laslett, Cambridge: Cambridge University Press

Lyons, David (1965). *Forms and Limits of Utilitarianism*, Oxford: Oxford University Press

Mill, John Stuart (1991). *On Liberty and Other Essays*, edited by John Gray, Oxford: Oxford University Press

Mitchell, George et al. (1993). 'Judgements of Social Justice: Compromises between Equality and Efficiency', *Journal of Personality and Social Psychology*, 65, 629–39

Moore, G. E. (1903). *Principia Ethica*, Cambridge: Cambridge University Press

Nozick, Robert (1974). *Anarchy, State, and Utopia*, Oxford: Basil Blackwell

Nagel, Thomas (1970). *The Possibility of Altruism*, Princeton: Princeton University Press

Nagel, Thomas (1991). *Equality and Partiality*, New York: Oxford University Press

Nagel, Thomas (1999). 'The Rigorous Compassion of John Rawls. Justice, Justice Shalt Thou Pursue', *New Republic*, 221, 17, 25 October 1999

Noddings, Nel (2002). *Starting at Home: Caring and Social Policy*, Berkeley: University of California Press

Nussbaum, Martha (2001). 'The Enduring Significance of John Rawls', *The Chronicle of Higher Education*, July 20 2001

Okin, Susan (1989). *Justice, Gender, and the Family*, New York: Basic Books

Parfit, Derek (1984). *Reasons and Persons*, Oxford: Oxford University Press

Putnam, Robert (2000). *Bowling Alone: the Collapse and Revival of American Community*, New York and London: Simon & Schuster

Richardson, Henry and Weithman, Paul (1999). *The Philosophy of Rawls: a Collection of Essays*, New York & London: Garland, Volumes 1–5

Rogers, Ben (2002). 'John Rawls – Obituary', *The Guardian*, November 27 2002

Ross, W. D. (1988). *The Right and the Good*, Indianapolis: Hackett

Sandel, Michael (1998). *Liberalism and the Limits of Justice*, Revised Edition, Cambridge: Cambridge University Press

Sen, Amartya (1999). *Development as Freedom*, Oxford: Oxford University Press.

Williams, Bernard (1985). *Ethics and the Limits of Philosophy*, London: Fontana

Wolff, Jonathan (1991). *Robert Nozick: Property, Justice, and the Minimal State*, Oxford: Basil Blackwell

Wolff, Robert Paul (1977). *Understanding Rawls: a Reconstruction and Critique of 'A Theory of Justice'*, Princeton: Princeton University Press

Glossary

Basic structure   Those social and economic institutions to which the principles of justice directly apply. Although the boundaries of the basic structure are vague, the idea is that such institutions fundamentally affect a person's life-chances.

Burdens of judgement   The sources, or causes, of disagreement between reasonable people.

Chain connection   The maximization of each income class consistent with maximizing the income of the least favoured class.

Circumstances of justice the social and economic conditions under which it is appropriate to apply principles of justice; the most significant of the circumstances of justice is moderate scarcity.

Closed society   A society entered at birth and exited at death. Agents in the original position assume they are choosing principles of justice for such a society.

Close-knitness   Maximizing the income of the least favoured class will, as a matter of empirical observation, tend to improve the prospects of the next class up the income scale.

Comprehensive conception of the good   The ends a person pursues and which give his life meaning, a religious belief and practice system being an example.

Comprehensive liberalism   Liberalism which draws on ideas that extend beyond the 'political' to include ideas about the nature of the human subject, or human rationality.

Constructivism (or **Kantian Constructivism**)   The idea that the validity of principles derives from a choice (or construction) procedure. Constructivism presupposes a complex conception of the human agent.

Democratic equality   Rawls's favoured interpretation of fair equality of opportunity, its chief characteristic being that it entails the rejection of the idea that opportunities should reflect the distribution and exploitation of natural talents.

Difference principle   Income, and other primary goods, should be distributed such that any inequalities are to the benefit of the least favoured class.

Domestic justice   The distribution of benefits and burdens within a single society – domestic justice focuses on the relationship between the individual and the state.

Envy (and **non-enviousness**)   A person's desire to limit differentials between himself and others (Rawls assumes that agents in the original position are non-envious).

Equal liberty principle   Each person is to enjoy an equal scheme of basic liberties.

Fair equality of opportunity   The first part of the second principle: it is open to four interpretations (see **democratic equality**, **liberal equality**, **natural aristocracy** and **natural liberty**).

Formal conception of right   The features which any moral principle should have apart from any substantive content, an example being publicity.

General conception of justice   An underlying idea of justice rather than specific principles: Rawls's favoured general conception is that a distribution should benefit the least favoured in society.

Ideal historical process   Rawls attributes this idea to Locke and Nozick: if each transaction is just, then the entire chain of transactions must be just.

Ideal social process   Against Locke and Nozick, Rawls argues that each transaction could in itself be just but the chain of transactions unjust. Justice is, in part, an attribute of the overall process.

Ideal theory (and **non-ideal theory**)   The assumption that people comply strictly with principles of justice and therefore we build a theory around that assumption (non-ideal theory does not rest on that assumption: civil disobedience, punishment, humanitarian intervention and immigration fall under non-ideal theory).

Imperfect procedural justice   We have an end which we aim to achieve (or perfect) but the procedure might fail to achieve it. An example is a criminal trial (see also **perfect procedural justice** and **pure procedural justice**).

Just savings principle   The requirement that we set aside resources for future generations.

Legitimate expectations   Individuals' behaviour is affected by what they understand to be the public rules of justice. For example, if a person knows that certain income levels attract a certain level of taxation then he can have no complaint if that amount of money is taken from his pre-taxed income.

Lexical ordering   A higher-level principle must be fully satisfied before we move to a lower-level one: the equal liberty principle is lexically prior to fair equality of opportunity, and fair equality of opportunity is lexically prior to the difference principle.

Liberal equality   An interpretation of fair equality of opportunity: unmerited advantages should, as far as possible, be removed.

Life-plan   We assume human beings are capable of conceiving of their lives as stretched out over time and so they will plan accordingly.

Maximax   Agents in the original position might choose to maximize their possible income by ensuring that the rich are as rich as possible (see **maximin**).

Maximin   Agents in the original position will, Rawls argues, choose to maximize the income of the poorest in society in case they end up in that class.

Mutual disinterest   Agents in the original position do not take an interest in each other's lives.

Natural aristocracy   An interpretation of fair equality of opportunity: the naturally favoured (the 'aristocracy') have a duty (*noblesse oblige*) to ensure the naturally unfavoured are taken care of.

Natural liberty   An interpretation of fair equality of opportunity: there must be equal access, meaning no sexual or racial discrimination, but natural and socially derived advantages are not nullified.

Original position   The imaginary situation in which agents choose principles of justice (see **veil of ignorance**).

Overlapping consensus   The justificatory basis for principles of justice: individuals converge on those principles from diverse religious and philosophical perspectives.

Partial compliance (and **strict compliance**) see **ideal theory**.

Perfect procedural justice   The procedure guarantees (perfects) an end: agreeing that the person who cuts the cake takes the last piece guarantees an equal division of the cake.

Political liberalism   The name for a theory of liberalism justified by restriction to a limited, and supposedly uncontroversial, set of values and concepts (see also **comprehensive liberalism**).

Primary goods   Short-hand for **social primary goods**.

Pure procedural justice   There is no criterion for determining what justice is beyond the procedure itself.

Rationality (or the **rational**)   The ability to institute and revise a life-plan: essentially, rational self-interest.

Reasonable pluralism   The situation in which individuals disagree but recognize that those with whom they disagree can reasonably hold the beliefs they do.

Reasonableness (or the **reasonable**)   The desire and willingness to live by moral principles (in contrast to, but not incompatible with, the rational).

Reflective equilibrium   The method by which the principles of justice are tested against everyday moral intuitions until principles and intuitions agree with one another and are in equilibrium

Representation   Agents in the original position are representatives of real people, although they do not know the identities of those they represent (see **veil of ignorance**).

Social primary goods   The all-purpose means to the realization of our ends: freedom, income and the bases of self-respect. (Natural primary goods are the things we are born with: health, strength, intelligence and so on.)

Special conception of justice   A particular specification of a more general conception of justice (see **general conception of justice**): the two principles constitute a special conception.

Stability   Political institutions are stable if their operation over time encourages adherence to them and discourages violation of them.

Strains of commitment   Recognition of the challenges on real people of living by the principles chosen by agents in the original position – those agents must take account of the strains of commitment when choosing principles.

Thin theory of the good   The agents in the original position must value something, and these are the (social) primary goods.

Veil of ignorance   The main feature of the original position: we choose principles without knowing our identities. We do have general knowledge of society.

Well-ordered society   A society in which people are willing to live by, and know others are willing to live by, principles of justice.

Index